Awakening The Mediumship Mind

The Psychology of Authentic Mediumship

Cameron Bayliss

FORWARD

There are books about mediumship that focus on techniques, others on personal stories, and many that try to prove to the world that spirit exists. This is not one of those books.

This is a book that dares to explore the truth beneath the gift, the emotional landscapes, the psychological weight, and the soul-altering journey of what it truly means to live as a medium. It is a work for those who do not just want to speak to the dead, but who long to understand why the dead still speak. It is a book for those who have felt the trembling in their chest before a message is born, who have held the grief of strangers as if it were their own, who have questioned their minds, their worth, their role. It is for those who have found healing not just in what they channel, but in who they become along the way.

I believe the path of the medium is one of the most sacred and demanding roles a human soul can undertake. Not because it is rare. But because it is deeply human. Mediumship asks us to walk with one foot in this world and one foot in the next, to hold space for the living and the dead with equal care, and to become a bridge, not just between people and their loved ones, but between psychology and spirit, silence and voice, shadow and light.

This book was born from the trenches of that walk. It was not written to impress. It was written to tell the truth. About grief. About trauma. About healing. About what it feels like to be both called and cracked open. It is a work that refuses to separate the soul from the nervous system, the mystical from the emotional, or the message from the medium. Because in truth, they are never separate. Every message is filtered through the human vessel. And if we are to serve with integrity, we must understand that vessel, its pain, its power, and its potential.

To every medium who has ever felt overwhelmed by the weight of what they carry, this book is for you. To every reader who is still trying to reconcile their spiritual gifts with their human wounds, may this work offer you a language you have long needed. To those who have never quite fit the mold, who feel too sensitive, too strange, too emotional, you are not broken. You are becoming.

It is my hope that as you move through these chapters, you will begin to see your path not as a performance or a burden, but as a sacred integration. That you will come to trust that your mediumship is not only a gift for others, but a map home to yourself. And that you will remember, again and again, that you are not here to be perfect. You are here to be present.

Welcome to the deep work. Welcome to the beautiful ache. Welcome to the lifelong path of being a medium.

Welcome home.

Contents

About the Author

Cameron Bayliss is a 6th Dimensional Medium, visionary teacher, and soul-based author whose work bridges the realms of spirit, psychology, and sacred transformation.

Known for his raw honesty and deeply intuitive approach, Cameron channels wisdom from higher dimensional guides while holding space for the emotional and ancestral layers of the human experience. His teachings awaken the mediumship mind, honour the wounded healer, and guide others toward truth, embodiment, and remembrance.

1. The Medium and the Mind

The art of mediumship is often regarded as mysterious and transcendent, something otherworldly that transcends logic and the rational mind. But at its core, mediumship does not bypass the human experience. It is deeply enmeshed within it.

The more a medium understands the human psyche, the more accurate, sensitive, and profound their connection to the spirit world becomes.

A medium is not simply a conduit between the living and the dead.

A medium is a finely attuned vessel of memory, emotion, trauma, intuition, and compassion. The psyche and the spirit are not opposites. They are mirrors of each other. To understand the dead, one must understand the living. To interpret the messages of spirit, one must be fluent in the language of grief, loss, guilt, shame, love, longing, and healing.

Mediumship begins not in the heavens, but in the heart and mind of a human being who dares to listen with every cell of their being.

The mind of a medium is rarely still. It is constantly taking in unspoken emotion, subtle energies, physical sensations, and fragmented impressions.

Many mediums have been sensitive from a young age, absorbing the moods of those around them, often feeling overwhelmed in crowds or emotionally saturated by other people's unexpressed pain. This sensitivity is not a weakness. It is the foundation of the gift.

The same nervous system that once registered danger or emotional abandonment is now a tuning fork for spiritual frequencies.

In truth, many mediums are trauma survivors, and their finely tuned systems have adapted not just to survive, but to sense.

When the medium learns to regulate this sensitivity and ground their awareness, what once caused confusion or anxiety becomes the very mechanism that allows accurate communication with spirit.

There is a neurological and psychological basis for this sensitivity.

The vagus nerve, the seat of the parasympathetic nervous system, plays a crucial role in emotional and energetic regulation. A dysregulated nervous system can lead to hypervigilance, anxiety, and emotional overload. But when it is understood and soothed, the medium can enter deep states of receptivity and trust.

The mind becomes a vessel, not a judge. The heart becomes an antenna, not a battleground. The body becomes a sacred witness to truth. This integration of mind, body, and spirit is not only essential for accurate mediumship, but also for the well-being of the medium.

Psychological self-awareness also improves discernment.

A medium who has not done their inner work may mistake projection for perception. They may hear their own fears or wounds echoed in the voices of spirit. They may unconsciously colour the message with their own beliefs or unresolved grief. But a medium who knows their own story, who has sat with their inner child, who has faced their shadow, becomes a clearer channel. They know the difference between what is theirs and what is not. They do not rush to interpret. They listen. They ask questions. They wait. They trust.

This is where the practice of self-inquiry becomes a sacred part of mediumship. Just as a therapist must examine their countertransference and personal triggers, so must a medium examine their emotional reactions during a reading. If a message brings up tears, is it because the client is grieving, or because the medium themselves has unresolved sorrow?

If a spirit feels aggressive or chaotic, is this the energy of the deceased, or is it an echo of the medium's past trauma? These questions are not asked to invalidate the experience, but to clarify it. The more self-aware the medium becomes, the more ethically and accurately they can serve the spirit world and the living.

In many ways, the path of the medium mirrors the path of the psychologist, the healer, and the wounded sage. It is a path of learning how the mind constructs meaning, how the body stores emotion, and how the soul seeks reconciliation.

Mediumship is not simply a mystical act. It is an act of deep psychological empathy.

The messages a medium receives often speak directly to the unconscious material of the client. A departed parent may bring forward the words the client never heard but longed for. A child in spirit may come not just to say goodbye, but to reassure the mother that the guilt she carries is not hers to bear. A grandparent may whisper the truth about a family secret, not to cause pain, but to break the silence that has passed down through generations.

These are not random messages. They are direct invitations into healing.

Understanding psychology allows the medium to hold these moments with skill and care. Trauma-informed awareness becomes vital. A medium who understands the nervous system, the nature of trauma, and the psychology of grief will know how to speak truth without causing harm. They will recognize when to pause, when to soften, when to offer space. They will understand that the reading is not about performance or impressing the sitter. It is about facilitating a sacred moment of reunion, truth, and release.

The mind of the client is also a key part of the mediumship experience. A person may come to a reading full of expectations, fears, scepticism, or hope. Their psychological state influences how they receive the message. A client who is in deep grief may only hear what they are emotionally ready to hear. A client who is shut down by trauma may intellectually grasp the message but be unable to emotionally integrate it.

A medium who understands these psychological defences can adjust their language and energy accordingly. They can hold the space with patience and compassion, allowing the message to settle over time rather than forcing immediate understanding.

This is why true mediumship is never just about what is said. It is about what is felt. It is about the energy behind the words. It is about the silent resonance between spirit, medium, and client. A message may seem simple on the surface, "She forgives you," "He is at peace," "They are proud of you", but beneath that simplicity lies a universe of unspoken emotion. A medium must feel this and allow the space for the client to receive it not just with their ears, but with their soul.

Mediumship is a mirror, reflecting back to the client what their psyche is ready to see.

It is also a mirror for the medium, constantly revealing where their own wounds still live.

Every reading is an invitation to deeper self-awareness. If a medium is triggered by a spirit, they must ask why. If a message feels blocked, they must explore what part of themselves may be afraid to receive it. This is not self-doubt. This is sacred inquiry. It is how the mind of the medium becomes a servant to truth rather than a filter of distortion.

Many mediums report that their own healing journey is what awakened their abilities. After loss, illness, trauma, or spiritual crisis, they became more attuned to subtle energies. Their minds, once full of defence mechanisms and distractions, became quiet enough to hear the whispers of the other side.

This is no coincidence. When the psyche breaks open, the spirit can enter. When the mind lets go of control, the heart becomes the compass. Mediumship, then, is not just a skill. It is a way of being. It is the result of integration, surrender, and trust.

To walk this path with integrity, a medium must continually study both spirit and self. They must be students of the soul and of psychology. They must understand grief, attachment, trauma, memory, and the complex architecture of the human mind.

They must understand projection, transference, and emotional regression. These are not clinical terms alone. They are living dynamics within every reading. A message from a father in spirit may trigger an abandonment wound. A sign from a late spouse may reopen unspoken resentment. A visit from a lost child may awaken both comfort and despair. The medium must know how to hold these paradoxes without collapsing into them.

The more psychologically aware a medium becomes, the more grounded their spiritual insight becomes. They do not confuse fear with intuition. They do not avoid hard truths in favour of comfort. They do not manipulate with vague sentimentality. Instead, they walk the middle path that is grounded in the human world, open to the spirit world, and anchored in the heart. They understand that spirit communication is not a performance, but a sacred conversation between realms.

In this chapter, we begin to see the true foundation of a medium's work.

It is not only about connecting to the dead. It is about understanding the living.

It is about healing the split between mind and spirit. It is about honouring the psychological terrain that gives shape to every message. The more you understand the human mind, the more clearly you hear the voice of spirit. The more you listen to your own soul, the more accurately you can serve others.

Mediumship is not separate from psychology. It is psychology extended into the unseen, the unfinished, and the eternal.

This is the work of the sacred messenger. Not to escape the mind, but to illuminate it. Not to bypass pain, but to walk with it. Not to speak for the dead alone, but to bring the living back to life.

Reflection Questions: The Medium and the Mind

1. In what ways has my emotional history shaped how I receive and interpret spirit communication?

2. How does my nervous system respond during a mediumship connection and what might this reveal about my internal state?

3. Where do fear, doubt, or past trauma still influence my ability to trust the messages I receive?

4. Do I allow space for both my human emotions and my spiritual role, or do I suppress one to uphold the other?

5. When I sit in silence, what voices arise from within; are they spirit, ego, memory, or something unresolved?

6. How do I maintain psychological grounding before, during, and after delivering a message from spirit?

7. What role has ancestral memory or inherited trauma played in the development of my intuitive and mediumistic abilities?

8. In what moments has my own healing deepened my mediumship and where is the next layer of healing calling me?

9. How do I balance ethical responsibility with emotional sensitivity when holding space for someone else's grief or trauma?

10. Am I using mediumship to perform, to heal, to serve, or to feel worthy and how might my intentions need to evolve?

2. Chapter Two: Mediumship as a Human Experience

Mediumship is most often described in spiritual terms. It is associated with the unseen, the celestial, and the mysterious. It is seen as a gift that rises above ordinary experience, connecting the living with the realm of the dead.

In truth, however, mediumship is not simply a spiritual ability. It is a deeply human experience. It is not only about speaking to spirits or receiving signs from the other side. It is about bearing witness to love, grief, guilt, forgiveness, and memory. It is about what it means to be human in a world where everything we love eventually changes or dies.

At the core of every mediumship reading is a relationship, a story, a longing for connection. The spirit world does not exist in isolation. It reflects the emotional and psychological reality of those still living. The medium becomes the bridge not only between two worlds, but between two emotional truths, the unfinished stories of the dead and the open wounds of the living.

Every person who sits before a medium brings with them a hidden library of emotion. There are words they never said. Regrets they never resolved. Love they never received. Questions they never asked and behind those questions are the deep, human needs that never fade, the need to be seen, to be forgiven, to be comforted, to be reassured.

These needs are not weaknesses. They are the very fabric of the human soul. When someone reaches out to a medium, they are not simply hoping for a paranormal experience. They are asking for an emotional connection. They are seeking a deeper understanding of what their loss means, what their connection still holds, and whether something sacred still binds them to those they loved and felt have lost.

In this way, mediumship is not a luxury. It is not entertainment. It is a sacred form of emotional care. It offers people something they rarely find in other places: a space where their love, their grief, and their questions are not dismissed or avoided, but honoured. In many cases, it is the only space where a person feels truly allowed to express their feelings about death. In modern society, grief is often hidden.

We are told to move on. We are praised for our strength when we suppress our sorrow. The dead are spoken about in hushed tones. Emotions are buried beneath distractions. But in a mediumship session, those barriers fall away. Tears are welcome. Longing is valid. Pain is understood and, in that vulnerability, healing becomes possible.

The human experience is not linear. It is cyclical. Love and loss weave through one another like vines. A person may have moved forward in life, but a part of them still waits at the grave of a loved one, hoping for one more moment, one more message, one more sign.

Mediumship does not erase this longing. It honours it. It meets it with compassion. It allows the grieving soul to remember that the love they feel is not in vain. It still lives. It still moves. It still reaches across worlds.

Spirits rarely speak in absolutes. They speak in emotion, in memory, in symbols that carry the weight of human experience. A grandmother may show an image of fresh bread because it reminds the family of how she cared for them. A child may flash the sound of a familiar laugh, or the memory of a toy, not because it is trivial, but because it is sacred.

These messages are not proof in the scientific sense. They are proof in the emotional sense. They validate that love continues. They affirm that nothing real is ever lost. They reconnect the living to the parts of themselves they had to bury along with the body of the person they loved.

The medium, in turn, must be more than a messenger. They must be a witness. They must know how to sit with sorrow without trying to fix it. They must understand the depth of human emotion without being overwhelmed by it. They must carry the presence of someone who can hold both the ache of separation and the hope of reunion at the same time.

This requires maturity. It requires empathy. It requires a deep respect for the complexity of grief.

Every mediumship reading is a conversation between stories. The story the client holds about the one they lost. The story the spirit carries about their life and death. The story that remains unfinished. The medium does not invent the story. They do not control the narrative. They step into it as a sacred listener, interpreting the symbols, feelings, and impressions that come through with care. They are not translators of language. They are translators of emotion.

And they must walk this path with reverence.

Many people come to mediumship when they are in crisis. They are raw, unsure, spiritually seeking, and emotionally exposed. They may not know what they need, only that they cannot carry their grief alone. Some come with guilt, wondering if their loved one is angry or disappointed. Some come with fear, worried that the death meant something they missed. Some come with disbelief, not sure whether to trust the process and any or all of these responses are deeply human.

A skilled medium will never shame or judge these emotions. Instead, they will meet them with openness. They will allow the client to feel safe enough to unfold, to release, to ask the questions they have been holding inside.

This safety is not only emotional. It is spiritual. The presence of spirit in a reading often brings a calm that cannot be explained. The atmosphere shifts. Time slows down. A hush comes over the room. And within that space, something ancient takes place. A remembering. A reunion. A reconnection to what is eternal.

Mediumship reminds the client that they are not crazy for still talking to their loved one. That they are not broken for still feeling them. That they are not weak for still grieving.

In this way, it affirms not just the spirit of the dead, but the spirit of the living.

Mediums are not immune to the human experience. They carry their own losses, their own doubts, their own healing journeys and in many cases, it is those very experiences that shape their sensitivity. A medium who has known the pain of loss can sit with a grieving parent in a way that is deeply authentic. A medium who has questioned their own beliefs can hold space for someone who is sceptical. A medium who has survived trauma can recognize the signs of emotional shutdown or spiritual fear.

These shared human experiences create a bridge between the medium and the client, and that bridge is what allows the message to land.

Mediumship also has the power to validate emotions that have been dismissed.

A woman may have been told to get over the death of her partner, but in the reading, the partner comes through with tenderness, acknowledging her daily pain and thanking her for carrying the love. A man may have hidden his tears for years, but when his father in spirit shows up with regret and love, the tears are finally allowed to flow.

This emotional validation is healing beyond words. It does not require belief. It only requires presence. The spirit sees. The medium hears. The client feels. And something sacred moves.

The humanity of mediumship also shows up in its imperfections. Messages may be subtle. Impressions may come in symbols. Not every detail is exact. Not every reading is crystal clear. But this too reflects the nature of life itself. Communication is not always precise. Emotions are not always tidy. Love is not always easy. In embracing the messiness, the medium honours the truth. Spirit does not speak in perfect sentences. It speaks in energy, in essence, in emotion and the medium's job is not to make it perfect, but to make it real.

At its deepest level, mediumship is not about information. It is about transformation.

A person walks into a reading with a heart full of questions, and they leave with a heart full of something else, sometimes peace, sometimes permission to grieve, sometimes a new connection to their own intuition. The experience does not end when the reading ends. It continues to ripple through their life, shifting their perspective, softening their pain, and reminding them that love cannot die.

In the most human terms, mediumship allows people to be seen. Not just as clients, but as souls. It allows them to lay down their masks and speak from the place of truth. It offers them a sacred mirror, not only reflecting the spirit of the one they lost but reflecting back to them the depth of their own love and capacity for healing.

It also reminds people that the relationship is not over. Just because someone has died does not mean the connection has ended. Love is not limited to the physical world. Spirit continues to communicate in dreams, in memories, in synchronicities, in the quiet spaces of the heart. A medium does not create that connection. They simply reveal what is already there. They help the client recognize the signs.

They remind them how to listen. They show them that they are not alone.

This is what makes mediumship a profoundly human experience. It is not about distance. It is about closeness. It is not about magic. It is about meaning. It is not about answers. It is about connection.

Every message, every impression, every moment of presence is a testament to the depth of human emotion and the eternal nature of love.

Mediumship does not require perfection. It requires presence. It requires a heart willing to feel, a mind willing to open, and a soul willing to serve. The medium stands not above the human experience, but within it. And from that place of humility and compassion, they become a channel, not only for spirit, but for healing.

To be a medium is to be a witness to the most sacred aspects of life and death. It is to hold the space where the veil thins and the heart opens. It is to speak the language of love, loss, and remembrance. And in doing so, it brings both the dead and the living back into the circle of belonging.

Reflection Questions: Mediumship as a Human Experience

1. How has mediumship changed the way I relate to my own life, relationships, and emotional patterns?

2. What part of my human story do I bring into every reading, consciously or unconsciously?

3. How do I honour my own emotions when I am constantly being asked to hold space for the emotions of others?

4. What does it feel like in my body when spirit is near, and how do I care for that body before and after?

5. Have I ever felt lonely on this path, and what part of me still longs for connection, understanding, or community?

6. In what ways has mediumship made me more compassionate toward human suffering, and where do I still resist that vulnerability?

7. How do I respond when my human self and my spiritual self seem to be in conflict?

8. What boundaries do I need to reinforce in my life to protect both my human wellbeing and my spiritual sensitivity?

9. When was the last time I felt truly alive, not just spiritually connected, but grounded, joyful, and fully human?

10. If I could speak to the version of me who first felt this calling, what would I say to them now, knowing everything I've lived through?

3. Ancestral Echoes

There is a presence that moves beneath the surface of every mediumship reading, subtle yet powerful. It is the quiet rhythm of ancestry, the pulsing memory of the bloodline, the echoes of lives lived long before our own.

While many mediumship sessions focus on recently departed loved ones, there is another layer that emerges through the work, a deeper current that reaches back through generations. This is where ancestral energy speaks. This is where unresolved family pain, generational patterns, and long-forgotten wounds rise to the surface. And this is where the medium is called to become more than a messenger. They become a healer of lineage, a witness to history, and a guide for the soul's deeper restoration.

Ancestral energy is not simply about biology. It is not limited to genetics or family trees.

It is the spiritual imprint of those who came before us, carried in the memory of our bones, our behaviours, our fears, and our inherited beliefs. Mediumship becomes a living bridge to this realm when spirit steps forward not just as an individual, but as a representative of an entire line. Grandparents and great-grandparents may show themselves in readings, but often they bring with them more than personal messages.

They carry the voice of those who never had one. They come to correct family myths, to speak the truth about events that were hidden, or to lift the weight of shame that was passed down in silence.

This is the domain of ancestral healing, and it is deeply intertwined with mediumship. The dead do not exist in isolation. They are part of a collective soul group that influences the living in unseen ways.

When a client sits before a medium, they may carry the weight of grief that is not theirs alone. They may be feeling sadness, guilt, fear, or confusion that belongs to someone in the family line, an unresolved trauma, an unspoken betrayal, or an identity that was suppressed or erased.

The medium, tuned in to this deeper level, may feel these emotions as if they are happening in the present moment and in a way, they are. Ancestral pain does not disappear with time. It lives on through behaviour, belief systems, and emotional patterns until it is acknowledged and healed.

Ancestral spirits often present themselves with a different kind of energy. There is a rootedness, an ancient presence, a sense of both distance and urgency. They are not always coming with affection or ease. Sometimes they come with heaviness.

Sometimes they carry sorrow. Sometimes they are seeking forgiveness for what they passed down. They may show the image of a child being separated from their mother. They may present a scene of war, exile, or poverty. They may speak in symbols, a broken locket, a torn letter, a burned photograph. These are not random images. They are the language of memory carried through blood.

Mediums who are open to ancestral work must be willing to listen on a deeper level. They must ask not only who the spirit is, but what they represent. Is this spirit a known relative, or an echo of a forgotten soul who was excluded from the family story? Is this a direct message to the client, or a generational request for healing?

In many cases, the spirit does not ask to be remembered as an individual but asks for the family to remember the truth. The truth of what was endured. The truth of what was denied. The truth of what still lingers in the emotional field.

These readings can be emotional and transformative. A woman may learn that her lifelong anxiety is connected to the suppressed grief of her great-grandmother, who lost several children and never spoke of them. A man may discover that his feelings of rage and abandonment are inherited from a grandfather who was sent away as a child and never fully returned to himself. A person may realize that their recurring dreams are not fantasies, but memories of a life lived by someone in their ancestral line.

In each of these cases, the spirit does not come to blame. They come to free. They come to bring understanding, and with that understanding, the possibility of change.

Mediumship that includes ancestral healing becomes a sacred act of repair. It is not about fixing the past but about acknowledging it. It is about offering presence and love where there was once neglect and silence.

The medium, by validating the presence of these older spirits, gives voice to those who were forgotten. They become the conduit for truths that could not be spoken in life. This kind of work is particularly powerful when it intersects with cultural or historical trauma, immigration, slavery, genocide, colonization, and systemic oppression. In these cases, the spirit world becomes a chorus of witnesses, and the medium becomes a sacred historian.

There is a reason why many indigenous and traditional cultures include ancestor veneration as part of their spiritual practice. These cultures understand that healing is not individual. It is collective.

The soul does not exist in isolation. It is braided into a lineage that stretches across time and space. When the ancestors are honoured, when their pain is acknowledged and their gifts are remembered, the living become more whole. They are no longer carrying pain they do not understand. They are no longer repeating patterns without knowing their origin. They begin to walk forward with a sense of connection and purpose. The role of the medium is to restore this awareness.

Sometimes ancestral spirits show up simply to say thank you. They acknowledge the living family member who broke a pattern, ended a cycle, or brought light to a story that was hidden in shame. These spirits may not have spoken in life, but in death they offer praise. They wrap their energy around the medium and client with deep gratitude. They say, "Because of you, the line will be different."

These are some of the most powerful moments in a mediumship session. They remind us that healing does not end with one lifetime. It moves backward and forward through the family tree, touching everyone who is connected.

Mediums who work with ancestral energy must also be prepared to hold the complexity of this realm. Not all ancestors were kind. Some carry the energy of abuse, violence, addiction, or betrayal. These spirits may show up with regret, or they may show up with confusion. Some may not be ready to acknowledge the harm they caused. Others may be filled with sorrow and want to make amends.

The medium must know how to hold these energies without judgment, without fear, and without becoming emotionally entangled. They must become a neutral vessel through which healing can begin.

It is important to remember that ancestral healing through mediumship is not about glorifying the past. It is about bringing truth to it. It is about allowing the spirit world to reveal the stories that shaped the soul of the family. It is about moving from silence to voice, from shame to acceptance, from pain to purpose.

The medium is not rewriting history. They are allowing the full spectrum of that history to be seen and felt and in doing so, they help the client step into their own life with a greater sense of clarity and empowerment.

One of the most extraordinary things about ancestral mediumship is that it often awakens the client's own intuition. Once they hear the story, once they feel the truth, something within them clicks into place. They begin to see patterns in their family. They remember the things that were whispered but never explained. They recognize the faces in old photographs with new eyes.

The work of the medium does not end in the reading. It begins a ripple effect through the client's awareness, offering insight, release, and a renewed connection to who they are and where they come from.

This kind of healing is also deeply embodied. The client may feel physical sensations during or after the session, warmth, release, tears, or even a feeling of emptiness as the weight begins to lift. This is because ancestral trauma is not just emotional. It is cellular. It lives in the nervous system, the organs, the subconscious.

When a medium facilitates ancestral release, the body often responds. It exhales. It softens. It begins to repair.

The medium too may feel the effects. Working with ancestral energy requires grounding, self-care, and deep energetic boundaries. The stories that come through can be intense. The emotions may be layered and heavy. The medium must have the capacity to process what they feel without carrying it.

This is why a personal practice of clearing, resting, and spiritual hygiene is essential. The medium must remain a clear and compassionate vessel, not absorbing the energy, but transforming it into understanding and peace.

There is something profoundly humbling about ancestral mediumship. It reminds us that we are part of something much larger than ourselves. That the pain we carry may not be ours to begin with, but that we have the power to transform it.

In the quiet space between words, in the subtle impressions that come through the veil, the ancestral realm speaks. It does not shout. It does not rush. It whispers. It offers fragments, images, and emotions. And if the medium is listening, truly listening, they will hear it. They will hear the stories that were silenced. They will feel the sorrow that was swallowed. They will sense the courage it took to survive. And they will bring that into the light.

Ancestral echoes are not just remnants of the past. They are invitations to remember who we are. They are bridges between worlds. They are calls to return to the roots of our being and to bring healing not just to ourselves, but to the entire line. Through the sacred art of mediumship, echoes become voices. These memories become messages and in the space between spirit and soul, the family becomes whole once more.

Reflection Questions: Ancestral Echoes

1. What ancestral stories or patterns have been passed down through my family, spoken or unspoken that still live within me?

2. In what ways have I inherited not only traits, but wounds, fears, or unresolved emotions from those who came before me?

3. Do I feel a spiritual connection to a particular ancestor, culture, or lineage? What messages or lessons arise from that connection?

4. How might ancestral trauma be shaping my nervous system, my worldview, or the way I serve others as a medium?

5. Have I ever felt a presence during a reading that felt older than the spirit being communicated, a lineage, a voice beyond time?

6. What rituals, practices, or quiet moments help me feel closest to my ancestors and the wisdom they carry?

7. Are there family patterns I am here to break and how does my mediumship offer a pathway to healing those cycles?

8. What ancestral gifts, strengths, or spiritual abilities have I reclaimed through my own healing journey?

9. When I look at the wounds I carry, how many of them feel like echoes rather than something I personally experienced?

10. How does honouring my ancestry deepen my relationship to spirit, self, and the unseen world?

4. The Psychology of Death

Death is a universal experience, and yet it remains the most avoided, misunderstood, and repressed subject in human society. It is the one certainty that every living being must face, and still, it is cloaked in fear, denial, and emotional distance.

For the medium, death is not an abstract event or a clinical moment. It is the threshold between this world and the next. It is the catalyst for connection, the foundation of the work and yet, to truly understand death as a medium, one must first understand the psychology of death, the way human beings process, defend against, and ultimately seek meaning through the experience of loss.

The mind does not approach death with neutrality. It resists it. It attempts to explain it, control it, delay it, or wrap it in comforting stories. From the moment we are old enough to understand that life is finite, the fear of death begins to shape our thoughts and behaviours. This fear is not always conscious. It can live in the background, subtly influencing our decisions, our relationships, and our beliefs.

We avoid the subject in conversation. We tell children that their grandparents went to sleep or became angels. We sanitize the language and dress it in euphemisms because the raw truth is too confronting for most. But mediums walk into this territory every day. They face what others avoid. They speak with those who have crossed that final threshold and in doing so, they become mirrors for the unspoken fears and emotions of the living.

Grief, denial, anger, bargaining, and acceptance are not just theoretical stages. They are psychological processes that often unfold in unpredictable and nonlinear ways. A medium must be fluent in this emotional language.

When a person seeks a reading, they are rarely doing so from a place of emotional neutrality. They are often caught somewhere between despair and hope. They may want closure, or they may want permission to keep grieving. They may be seeking answers they could not face while their loved one was still alive. In these moments, the medium is not just communicating with spirit. They are walking beside a human being whose psyche is navigating one of the most vulnerable passages of life.

Understanding how people psychologically respond to death allows the medium to hold space with compassion and clarity. Some clients are in the early stages of shock. They are numb, emotionally frozen, unable to access the deeper layers of feeling. Others may be deeply angry, especially if the death felt unjust, sudden, or avoidable.

Some carry guilt, whether rational or not. They believe they could have done more, said more, or prevented what happened. Others may be stuck in complicated grief, holding onto the pain because letting it go feels like letting go of the person they lost. All of these responses are deeply human. And all of them affect how a client hears and receives messages from spirit.

The psychological landscape of death is often shaped by personal and cultural beliefs. Some people fear judgment after death. Others believe in reincarnation. Some have been raised in strict religious environments where death is either a punishment or a reward.

Others have grown up in secular households where death is viewed as the end of consciousness. These beliefs shape the client's expectations and interpretations during a reading. A skilled medium will not impose their own beliefs. Instead, they listen. They attune to the emotional undertone of the client's words. They recognize that for some, the reading is not only about connecting to the spirit of a loved one, but about redefining their relationship with death itself.

Mediumship often brings forward truths that were hidden in life.

A spirit may reveal that they were not afraid when they died. That they were not alone. That they found peace in the final moments. These messages can be profoundly healing, especially for clients who carry traumatic images of how their loved one passed. The mind often replays the moment of death obsessively, filling in the blanks with fear and imagined suffering.

The medium, by offering the spirit's perspective, can interrupt this pattern. They can help the client replace horror with peace, uncertainty with understanding.

The psychology of death is not only about the one who has passed. It is also about those who remain. Death forces the living to confront their own mortality. It shakes the illusion of control. It exposes the fragile nature of time and the unpredictable flow of life.

For some, this becomes a spiritual awakening. For others, it becomes a crisis. The medium, standing in that sacred space between life and death, becomes a guide. Not by offering easy answers, but by embodying presence. By saying, with every fibre of their being, that it is safe to feel what has not been felt. That death is not an enemy. That the story does not end.

Many clients come to a medium seeking contact with someone whose death was complicated or unresolved. A suicide. An overdose. A death by violence or illness that unfolded over months of suffering.

These cases require immense care. The client may be carrying trauma, shame, confusion, or unanswered questions.

The medium must listen with every part of their being. They must resist the urge to rush into messages. They must hold the grief gently, allowing the spirit to communicate in their own way and time. In these moments, the medium is not only a messenger. They are a sacred witness to pain, a mirror to the depth of love that still endures.

Sometimes a spirit does not come through in a way the client expects. They may not apologize. They may not address the issue the client is fixated on. This can be difficult, especially if the death was surrounded by emotional turmoil. But even in this, there is meaning. The psychology of spirit communication is not about performance. It is about timing, healing, and soul truth. What is not said is often as important as what is.

The medium must be prepared to explain that not every spirit comes with clear answers. Some come simply with presence. Some offer peace, not explanations. Some come to say goodbye, others to say nothing at all. And all of this is valid.

The psychology of death also includes the phenomenon of unfinished business. Many people die with regrets. With things unsaid, actions undone, forgiveness not offered. These themes often emerge in mediumship. A spirit may acknowledge the harm they caused. They may offer insight into their own emotional limitations.

They may take responsibility for what they could not face while alive. This can be deeply healing for the client, especially if the relationship was strained. It can also be destabilizing. Hearing from a spirit who was once abusive or absent can reopen old wounds. The medium must be able to hold this with strength and compassion, never pushing forgiveness but creating space for it if the client is ready.

In other cases, it is the client who needs to say something. They need to express anger, sorrow, confusion, or even relief.

Mediumship can be a space where this expression is not judged. The spirit world is often more understanding than the human world. They receive the client's truth without ego, without defence. They hold space for the release of emotion, for the unburdening of the soul. This is why mediumship is not only about what comes from spirit. It is about what is expressed by the living. It is a two-way healing. A sacred dialogue.

Death often changes the identity of the living. A woman loses her husband and becomes a widow. A child loses a parent and becomes an orphan. A sibling loses their twin and feels as if half of themselves is missing. These identity shifts are not always understood or supported by society. But the medium sees them.

The medium recognizes the transformation. They see the grief not as a problem to solve but as a sacred rite of passage. They honour the soul who is grieving by acknowledging their pain, their love, and their courage.

The medium also carries their own relationship with death. Most mediums have experienced significant loss. It is often through that loss that their abilities awaken or deepen. Their understanding of death becomes personal, not theoretical. They know what it means to ache. They know what it means to wonder if the signs are real. They know what it feels like to long for one more message.

This shared humanity becomes the foundation of their work. It allows them to speak not from a place of authority, but from a place of empathy.

In a world where death is often denied or sterilized, the medium becomes a keeper of sacred truth. They bring death back into the realm of meaning, connection, and love. They show that death is not the end of the relationship. That love continues to speak. That the soul continues to evolve. That there is more to the story than what was written in the final chapter of a physical life.

The psychology of death, when embraced, becomes a doorway. It becomes an initiation into deeper feeling, deeper truth, deeper presence. Mediumship is not about escaping this reality. It is about illuminating it. It is about showing that the pain of death is not something to be feared or avoided, but something to be held with reverence. It is about allowing death to teach us how to live.

When the veil between worlds grows thin, the mind may struggle to understand what the heart already knows. That death is a threshold, not a wall. That grief is a testament to love. That the ones we lose are never truly gone. And that by facing death, we come closer to the sacredness of life.

The psychology of death is one of the most profound areas a medium must learn to understand, not only in terms of spirit communication, but as a reflection of the human psyche. Death is more than a biological ending; it is a psychological and spiritual transition.

For many, the fear of death is rooted not in dying itself, but in the unknown, in the perceived loss of identity, connection, and meaning. Mediums are often the bridge for those left behind, helping to bring peace, closure, and the understanding that death is not a disappearance but a transformation. To teach this, a medium must first explore their own relationship with death, what it stirs in them, what fears it awakens, and how their personal beliefs shape the way they hold space for others.

Grief, too, is not a linear process but a psychological landscape that shifts depending on personality, culture, spiritual beliefs, and the depth of love. As mediums, we witness the rawest forms of human emotion when a loved one has passed. Teaching about death must include teaching about grief, not just as sorrow, but as an expression of love and the reorientation of life after loss.

Students of Mediumship should be encouraged to see grief not as something to fix, but something to witness and honour. This shifts the role of the medium from one who "proves life after death" to one who helps others navigate the very human experience of mortality with reverence and gentleness.

It is also essential to address the psychological coping mechanisms people use in the face of death, denial, avoidance, anger, and even spiritual bypassing. A medium who teaches this work must be able to recognize when a client or student is not ready to hear from spirit because they are emotionally or psychologically ungrounded. Mediumship is not about forcing messages, it is about timing, readiness, and consent.

When we understand how trauma, unprocessed grief, or psychological fragility can shape someone's reaction to death, we become more ethical, compassionate practitioners. Teaching students to listen not just with their intuitive senses, but with psychological insight, makes them safer and more impactful.

Finally, teaching the psychology of death must include the sacred. We are not here to reduce death to a set of theories or fears, but to restore its spiritual meaning. Death is part of the soul's journey, and mediums are the sacred witnesses of that crossing. Death teaches us how to live more fully and when mediums understand the psychology beneath it, they become not just messengers of spirit, but stewards of healing in a world still learning how to face the end with grace.

Reflection Questions: The Psychology of Death

1. What was my first experience of death, and how did it shape the way I view mortality?

2. How do I personally define death, not just as a physical event, but as a spiritual and emotional transition?

3. What fears do I still carry around dying, losing someone I love, or what comes after?

4. When I sit with someone grieving, what emotions are triggered within me, do I try to fix, avoid, or fully feel?

5. How does my work as a medium influence how I process loss, grief, and my own impermanence?

6. What psychological defenses do I notice in myself when confronted with death, do I intellectualize, numb, spiritualize?

7. In what ways do I use mediumship to make sense of the unknown, and where do I still struggle to trust?

8. Have I truly allowed myself to grieve my past losses, or have I only moved forward intellectually?

9. What cultural or family beliefs about death shaped my early worldview, and do they still hold true for me?

10. How do I respond to the silence that death brings, both in others and within myself?

11. What does it mean to me to hold space for death, not just physically, but emotionally and energetically?

12. Where do I carry unresolved grief in my body, and how does it affect my connection to spirit?

13. What has death taught me about love and how has that changed the way I live?

14. When I deliver a message from someone who has passed, what part of my own humanity is touched in the process?

15. Can I sit with the mystery of death without needing all the answers or is there still something within me seeking control?

5. The Body Remembers

There is a wisdom in the body that language cannot reach. It is a silent archive that stores everything we have lived through, everything we have felt, and everything we have not yet healed.

For mediums, this embodied intelligence becomes a powerful instrument of communication. Messages from the spirit world do not always arrive as words or visions. They often emerge as sensations, subtle movements, shivers, nausea, sudden tears, or the overwhelming feeling of joy or sorrow that comes from nowhere.

The body becomes the first place where truth arrives, and it often speaks long before the conscious mind can translate it. In mediumship, the body is not just a vessel. It is the medium.

Every human being carries the imprint of their personal history in their physical form. Trauma, grief, love, and memory are etched into the nervous system. When we ignore these sensations, we become disconnected from ourselves and from spirit. But when we learn to listen, we open a new pathway of communication, one that does not rely on logic, but on presence. The body becomes a sacred tool for the medium, not only to receive spirit, but to interpret emotional truth, both their own and their client's.

A person who has not healed their relationship with their own body may struggle to be a clear channel. If they dissociate from physical sensation, numb emotional responses, or ignore the language of the body, they may block or misinterpret the messages that come through.

Many mediums are empathic, highly sensitive to the physical and emotional energy of others. This can be both a gift and a burden.

When a medium learns to attune to these signals without becoming overwhelmed, they begin to receive spirit communication with extraordinary accuracy and depth.

Sensations in the body during a reading are not random. They are part of the spirit's message. A sudden pain in the chest may indicate a heart attack. A tightness in the throat may point to something left unsaid. A tingling in the scalp or a wave of warmth across the shoulders may signal a benevolent presence. These sensations often last only a moment, but they carry precise information.

The medium who has trained themselves to notice, interpret, and speak these sensations aloud becomes a translator not just of words, but of energy.

Sometimes the body remembers things the mind has forgotten. This is especially true in ancestral mediumship and trauma-informed readings. A medium may suddenly feel anxious or heavy in a session without understanding why.

Upon further exploration, it may become clear that the client is carrying inherited grief, or that a spirit is attempting to share the emotional climate of their death. The medium's body mirrors the energy of the story.

This is why grounding, clearing, and releasing practices are essential. The medium must not hold these sensations beyond the session. They must become skilled in releasing what is not theirs.

The client's body is also part of the mediumship process. Many clients report feeling chills, pressure, tingling, or warmth during a session.

These responses are validations. They are the body's way of recognizing spiritual truth. When a client hears something that deeply resonates, they often tear up, their chest softens, their shoulders drop. These are signs of release. They may not consciously understand the message at first, but their body understands.

The nervous system reacts to truth with stillness, openness, and presence. The medium who observes these reactions knows when to pause, when to soften, and when to offer silence so the body can integrate what has just been received.

The science of trauma has revealed that unprocessed emotional experiences are stored in the body. The work of somatic psychologists shows that grief, fear, and unexpressed pain become held in the muscles, the breath, and the cellular memory. When spirit brings up these themes in a reading, the client's body often reacts. This is not something to fear. It is an opportunity for healing.

A spirit may come forward not just with words, but with an energy that helps to unlock frozen emotion. A reading, then, becomes more than communication. It becomes emotional release. The client may feel lighter, as though a weight has been lifted. This is not imaginary. It is a real physiological shift, triggered by the reactivation and resolution of long-held emotion.

The body also plays a role in how the medium connects with different types of spirits. A child spirit may make the medium feel small, gentle, or playful in their posture. A masculine spirit may bring a sudden sense of strength or confidence. A grandmother may trigger the sensation of warmth in the hands or the desire to rock back and forth.

These embodied reactions are not acting. They are intuitive mimicking. The spirit's energy is being translated through the physical channel of the medium, and the body becomes the stage upon which the essence of the spirit is felt and expressed.

During some readings, the body becomes the container for the unspoken. A client may not be able to speak their truth, but the medium feels it in their chest. A spirit may not use language but sends a vibration of emotion that lands in the stomach.

The medium learns to trust these moments. They do not dismiss them. They do not rush to explain them away. They sit in the silence of sensation, waiting until the message forms in the mind. This is the deeper work of mediumship, learning to speak what the body feels before the intellect interrupts.

For mediums who have experienced trauma, the body can be both a gateway and a challenge. Trauma often causes dissociation, a disconnection from the physical self. The medium may struggle to stay grounded during a reading.

They may leave the body during intense emotional exchanges, or they may suppress sensations that feel overwhelming. This is where healing work becomes essential. The more the medium reclaims their body, the more accurate and embodied their readings become.

Somatic practices such as breathwork, movement, grounding exercises, and trauma-informed therapy can help restore the connection between body and spirit. When the medium is fully present in their body, they become a more powerful and trustworthy vessel for the unseen.

Mediumship is not just a mental or spiritual act. It is a full-body experience.

The spirit world does not limit its communication to words and images. It uses every available channel, sound, feeling, movement, pressure, breath. The body of the medium becomes a sacred instrument. Like a tuning fork, it vibrates with the frequency of truth. Like an antenna, it receives signals that cannot be seen. Like a drum, it echoes the rhythms of the soul.

Even outside of readings, the medium's body often acts as a barometer for energy. They may feel heavy before a storm, restless before a death, or uplifted when a loved one is near. They may walk into a room and immediately sense the emotional tone. This sensitivity must be honoured and managed.

Without awareness and boundaries, the medium may absorb too much. With care and training, they learn to distinguish between what is theirs and what is coming from another. This discernment protects the medium's health and enhances their accuracy.

Spiritual hygiene for the body is just as important as clearing the mind. Salt baths, energy work, body scans, breathwork, and grounding rituals all support the physical aspect of mediumship. The body must be respected, rested, and nourished. If the medium neglects their physical health, the channel becomes unclear.

Fatigue, emotional burnout, and energetic congestion cloud the connection. The more the medium listens to their body, the more trustworthy their gift becomes.

In some cases, the body can also become the medium through which healing is transmitted. A medium who places their hand on the client's shoulder during a reading may unintentionally activate a wave of emotion. A moment of stillness may bring a spiritual download that enters not through words, but through presence. These moments are subtle, but profound. They remind us that healing is not always spoken. Sometimes it is felt.

The relationship between body and spirit is not separate. It is intimate. Spirit enters through breath, through stillness, through sensation. The body is not a distraction. It is a sacred ally. It is through the body that the medium learns to feel what cannot be seen, to speak what cannot be said, and to embody the presence of love and truth.

When a spirit wants to bring peace, the body of the medium relaxes. When a spirit wants to bring urgency, the body tightens. This can be a frightening experience for the Medium.

When a message is being blocked by fear or resistance, the medium may feel dizzy or disoriented. These are not problems. They are messages. The medium learns to become curious about these signals. They ask what the body is trying to say. They let the body lead.

The body is also where the spirit of the medium lives. It is where their own healing journey unfolds. The more they honour their physical form, the more access they have to spirit. Mediums who are embodied are mediums who are grounded, present, and trustworthy. They do not float above life. They walk within it. And it is this groundedness that makes their readings transformative.

The body remembers everything. The loss. The joy. The trauma. The love. And when the medium learns to speak from the body, they become the voice of all that was never said. They become the echo of truth. They become the sacred space where memory, presence, and spirit converge.

Mediumship is not only a gift of the mind or a skill of the soul. It is a wisdom of the flesh.

It is the willingness to feel what others have hidden. It is the courage to listen when the body trembles with emotion. It is the grace to allow tears, to allow shivers, to allow sensation to be the message itself. In this way, the medium becomes not just a translator of spirit, but a living embodiment of truth.

Reflection Questions: How the Body Remembers

1. When spirit is near or emotion arises in a session, where do I feel it most in my body and what might that sensation be telling me?

2. Are there parts of my body that feel heavy, tense, or numb during certain types of spirit communication or emotional moments?

3. What physical symptoms or recurring sensations have accompanied past trauma, and do they still appear in moments of spiritual connection?

4. How do I respond when my body signals exhaustion, overwhelm, or intuitive warning, do I listen or override?

5. In what ways has my body protected me from emotional or spiritual overwhelm in the past and am I still relying on those patterns?

6. What would it mean to treat my body not just as a vessel for spirit, but as a living record of everything I have survived, felt, and held?

6. Death Rituals and Spiritual Pathways

Throughout human history, death has never been merely an end. It has been a transition, a passage, and a profound moment of transformation. In every ancient culture, death was honoured with ceremony, prayer, and sacred ritual. The body was not discarded. It was anointed, dressed, blessed, and returned to the earth or the flames with intention. The soul was not banished. It was guided, honoured, and remembered.

These death rituals were not only for the deceased. They were also for the living. They offered structure to grief, meaning to mystery, and pathways for the soul to continue its journey beyond the veil. In the work of mediumship, these ancient truths still echo. The way the dead speak, the way they present themselves, and the way they linger or move on, all reveal the lasting impact of how they were treated in death.

Mediumship is deeply intertwined with ritual, even when the setting does not appear ceremonial. The process of sitting with someone who seeks connection with a loved one, opening the heart to receive the spirit world, and speaking messages from beyond the grave is a form of ritual. It is a sacred act.

When the medium becomes aware of the spiritual structures that surround death, they gain insight not only into the nature of the soul's journey, but also into the emotional and psychological healing of those left behind. Death rituals, whether formally practiced or spiritually remembered, shape the way a spirit returns, how they communicate, and why they linger.

In cultures where death is treated as sacred, spirits often come through with a sense of peace. They are grounded, complete, and carry a sense of closure. Their presence feels calm and resolved. In contrast, when death has been denied, suppressed, or surrounded by trauma and confusion, the spirit may appear with urgency, fragmentation, or heaviness.

They may not come to deliver a message, but to seek one. They may need validation, forgiveness, or acknowledgment that they did not receive at the time of their passing. In these moments, the medium becomes a surrogate ritualist, offering what the family or culture could not.

When a spirit shows the image of a candle, a prayer, or a sacred object, they are not making random symbols. They are recalling the moments that helped guide them home. In many readings, a spirit will express gratitude for the way they were laid to rest.

A simple act of singing to the body, holding their hand, or placing meaningful items near them during their passing can become deeply significant in the afterlife. These moments are carried with the soul. They are felt as bridges of love.

Mediums who are sensitive to this will often receive vivid impressions of these rituals and can confirm to the client what took place. This validation is powerful. It reassures the living that they did not fail. That what they offered was felt.

There are also times when rituals were absent. The person may have died alone, without prayer, without presence, without the touch of a loved one. This is especially true in cases of sudden death, hospital restrictions, or distant families. These spirits may express loneliness, confusion, or a desire to revisit the moment of passing with a sense of sacredness.

In such cases, the medium may guide the client in offering a symbolic ritual after the reading, lighting a candle, writing a letter, saying a prayer, or visiting a place that mattered. These acts, though simple, have immense spiritual weight. They create completion. They honour what was missing. They serve as a form of energetic restitution for the spirit and for the grieving heart.

The soul's journey after death is influenced by many factors. Belief systems, emotional state, cause of death, and the presence or absence of sacred support all affect the transition. Some spirits pass easily, surrounded by love. Others resist or delay, especially if they have unfinished business, unresolved guilt, or attachment to the material world.

Mediumship often reveals where the soul is on their path. Some spirits come from a place of light and clarity, bringing guidance and wisdom. Others come from closer to the earth, still finding their way. Neither is better or worse. They are simply in different stages of the journey. The medium must hold all of them with equal respect.

Many traditional cultures speak of psychopomps, beings, spirits, or practitioners who help guide the soul to the next world. In mediumship, this role still exists. The medium becomes a bridge, a helper, a companion who acknowledges the spirit's presence and gently reminds them they are not forgotten.

Sometimes, this recognition alone is enough to help the spirit move on. When a soul feels seen, they feel released. When they feel remembered, they feel real. The medium does not force them to move.

They honour where they are. But in doing so, they often facilitate the very peace the spirit was seeking.

Spiritual pathways after death are not linear. They are unique to the soul. Some spirits describe beautiful landscapes, gardens, light, and reunions. Others speak of reflection, learning, or healing centres where they rest and review their life. Some do not communicate much at all. They offer only presence, emotion, or subtle signs.

The medium must never assume. They must let the spirit show what is true for them. This diversity of experience mirrors the diversity of human life. Just as no two lives are the same, no two deaths are the same. And yet, across all messages, one truth remains: love continues.

When the living engages in ritual, even years after death, the spirit often responds. Acts of remembrance are powerful. Lighting a candle, speaking their name, making offerings, creating altars, singing songs, planting trees, these are not empty gestures. They are bridges. They call the spirit close. They create sacred space. They invite dialogue. Mediums can encourage these rituals as part of healing.

They empower clients to recognize that they can continue the relationship in meaningful ways. That they are not helpless. That the bond has not ended.

Grief rituals are especially important. Modern society often lacks structure for mourning. People are expected to return to normal life quickly, to hide their pain, to grieve in private. This repression creates emotional stagnation. Spirits often express frustration that their death was never fully honoured.

A funeral may have occurred, but the emotional ritual, the true acknowledgment of the bond was missing. Mediumship becomes a place where that ritual can begin. Tears, silence, touch, storytelling, breath, these become sacred acts in the presence of spirit. The medium holds space for the ritual to unfold organically. The words may not be poetic. The emotions may be raw. That is where the healing lives.

There are also cultural rituals that spirits may ask to be continued. A grandmother may want her grandchild to carry on a tradition. A father may wish to pass down a prayer, a craft, or a family recipe. These are not sentimental requests. They are legacies. The spirit is asking to remain part of the lineage through sacred continuity.

When a medium delivers such messages, they are not only connecting the client to their loved one, but they are also connecting the present moment to the ancestral web. They are reminding the client that they are part of a story much larger than themselves.

In some cases, spirits come to inspire new rituals. The client may be guided to create a practice that did not exist before. A monthly offering. A letter-writing ceremony. A walk in nature where they speak to their loved one aloud. These rituals are personal, but deeply effective. They help the soul integrate the loss and maintain the connection in a healthy way. The medium can act as a guide in this process, offering suggestions that resonate with the spirit's energy and the client's needs.

Mediumship itself becomes a modern ritual. It is often the first time the client has spoken openly about their grief. It may be the first time they have allowed themselves to feel the depth of their longing. The medium's words, the silence between them, the presence of spirit, all these elements combine to form a ceremonial space where healing can occur. When approached with reverence, a reading becomes as sacred as a funeral rite. It is a moment of communion between worlds.

The death rituals of ancient times were not only about the body. They were about the soul's passage. They guided the spirit with prayers, songs, symbols, and offerings. They told the dead they were safe, loved, and free to go. They told the living it was time to mourn, to remember, and eventually, to live again.

In the absence of these traditions, the modern medium must understand the psychological and spiritual void that often remains. By recognizing the importance of ritual, they help restore the balance between death and life, between loss and meaning.

When a spirit comes through clearly, when their presence is felt and their message is received, something shifts. A sense of peace enters the room.

The veil between worlds becomes soft. The client may feel a warmth in their chest, a sudden quiet in their mind. This is the residue of sacred connection. It is the presence of something ancient and holy. It is the moment when love reaches beyond time and space, reminding us that nothing is ever truly lost.

Ritual is not about superstition. It is about intention. It is about creating containers for emotion, meaning, and transformation. It is about giving the soul a pathway to move forward. For the medium, ritual is not always visible.

It lives in the breath before the message. In the silence after the tears. In the prayer whispered before the session begins. It lives in the way the medium honours the unseen. In the way they bow, internally, to both the spirit and the living. This inner ritual is what makes the work sacred.

As mediums, we must reclaim the power of ritual. Not in grand gestures, but in small acts of reverence. We must remind our clients that grief is not a disorder. It is a sacred response to love. We must remind them that their loved ones are not gone but transformed. That they can be spoken to, honoured, and walked with. That death is not an end. It is a passage, and we are the witnesses.

Reflection Questions: Death Rituals and Spiritual Pathways

1. What personal or cultural death rituals have shaped my beliefs about what happens after we die, and do they still resonate with me today?

2. In moments of loss, what spiritual practices or sacred acts have helped me process grief or feel connected to the spirit world?

3. How do I honour the souls I communicate with; do I create space for ritual, reverence, or acknowledgment beyond the message?

4. What death rituals would I want for myself, and what does that reveal about how I understand the soul's journey?

5. When I witness or facilitate a reading with a grieving person, how can I support the integration of spiritual connection with ritual healing?

6. In what ways does my mediumship act as a living ritual, a sacred practice that creates a pathway between this world and the next?

7. What role does sacred silence, music, nature, or symbolic objects play in the way I connect with spirit during moments of transition or remembrance?

8. How can I integrate meaningful death rituals into my mediumship practice to honour the dead, support the living, and deepen my spiritual path?

7. Grief as a Portal

Grief is often misunderstood. It is spoken of as something to get over, something to manage, something to survive. It is treated as a wound that should eventually close, a storm that will pass if we are strong enough.

But for mediums, grief is not a detour or an obstacle. It is a doorway. It is a sacred portal that opens the soul to a deeper realm of truth. Grief softens the barriers between this world and the next. It pulls back the illusion of permanence and reveals the invisible thread that still binds us to those we have lost.

Through grief, a person does not become weaker. They become open. They become more sensitive, more aware, more connected. Mediumship often begins in the shadow of grief. And in many ways, it is grief that prepares the heart for spirit.

When someone loses a loved one, they often experience a spiritual awakening that is not spoken of in conventional grief models. Something within them is shattered, but something else is stirred. They begin to feel the presence of the person they lost.

They sense them in dreams, in music, in the way the wind moves across their skin. They begin to look for signs, not because they are desperate or delusional, but because their heart has become attuned to a new frequency. The veil is thinner. The world is quieter. Grief has stripped away the noise, and what remains is a raw and open channel through which love still speaks.

This phenomenon is not limited to those who identify as psychic or spiritual. It happens to ordinary people every day. A grieving mother feels her child's arms around her at night. A man hears his wife's voice whispering in his ear just before he wakes. A daughter smells her father's cologne while sitting in his old chair. These are not fantasies. They are the subtle language of spirit.

Grief opens the body to sensation, the mind to memory, and the heart to presence. Mediums often say that the most powerful connections come through those who are still grieving, because their longing has become a bridge.

The soul that grieves is not broken. It is becoming. Grief dismantles the illusion that we are separate, and in that dismantling, we become more receptive to what is eternal. Mediumship becomes a form of alchemy, transforming sorrow into sacred connection.

The medium does not simply deliver messages. They step into the energetic field of grief and help the client feel the truth they already carry and that love is not bound by the body, that presence does not die with breath, that the relationship continues in new and mysterious ways.

For many mediums, their gift awakened through their own loss. They were not seeking it. It found them in the quiet aftermath of death. A parent, a child, a friend passed, and the world changed. In that change, something opened. The pain became a doorway through which spirit walked. The medium did not need to believe. They only needed to feel. What they felt was real. Grief became the teacher. The first lesson was heartbreak.

The second was presence. The third was the realization that death is not the opposite of life, but part of its eternal rhythm.

Clients often arrive in deep grief, unsure of what they believe, uncertain of what they are seeking. They come not for entertainment or proof, but for peace. They carry sorrow in their voice, in the way they sit, in the weight they hold behind their eyes. The medium does not rush to lift this sorrow. They do not try to fix or avoid it. They honour it. They make space for it. They recognize that grief is a sacred process, not a problem.

In this space of reverence, spirit is invited in and what emerges is not always words. Sometimes it is presence. A feeling of warmth. A sudden shift in the atmosphere. A breath that finally releases after being held too long.

Mediumship becomes the ritual grief never received. In a society that often denies or minimizes emotional pain, the reading offers validation. It allows the client to speak the name of their loved one, to remember, to cry, to feel. It allows them to experience something that defies explanation; a moment of connection that transcends the limits of time and death. This connection does not erase the grief. It deepens it. It makes it holy. It transforms it from something to endure into something to honour.

There is no one way to grieve. Some carry their pain quietly for decades. Others express it openly. Some need to ask questions. Others need to simply be held.

The medium learns to read these unspoken needs. They listen not only to the words, but to the body, the breath, the silence between phrases. They allow the grief to lead the way. If a client needs to cry for ten minutes before speaking, the medium holds that space. If the client begins to laugh through their tears, the medium does not correct them. Grief is complex. It contains every emotion. It is never clean, and, in its messiness, it is deeply human.

Spirit often meets the client in their grief with compassion. They do not rush or force. They bring symbols, memories, sensations that the client will recognize. A father may show the smell of the garden he tended. A sister may send the feeling of a shared childhood game. A child may communicate through the sound of laughter.

These small details carry enormous emotional weight. They say, "I am still here." They say, "I remember." They say, "Our love did not end." The client may burst into tears at these details, not because they are sad, but because they are seen.

Grief is not linear. It is not something we move through in neat stages. It rises and falls. It retreats and returns. It surprises us in the middle of joy. It softens only to sharpen again.

Mediums who understand this will never judge the client for how they are grieving. They will not try to bring closure. They will bring presence. They will honour the process as ongoing. Even if the loss occurred twenty years ago, the grief may still live in the body, waiting for a moment of recognition. The reading becomes that moment and what follows is often a profound sense of release.

For some, grief becomes a spiritual path. It opens questions that were never asked before. It stirs memories of ancestral rituals, intuitive knowing, or childhood sensitivities that were dismissed. The grieving person begins to feel more. To sense more. To notice signs. They become curious about what lies beyond. In this way, grief becomes the gateway to spiritual development.

The medium becomes a guide, not only to the departed, but to the client's own awakening. They help the client trust what they feel. They validate the signs, the dreams, the subtle communications that are already occurring.

This empowerment is a key part of the medium's role. The reading is not the end. It is the beginning. It is a reminder that the client can continue the relationship in their own way. They can speak to their loved one. They can write letters. They can listen in silence. They can create rituals of remembrance. They are not dependent on the medium. The medium has simply reminded them of what is already within.

Some forms of grief are complex. A person may grieve someone who caused them harm. A parent who was abusive. A sibling who was estranged. A partner who left behind chaos. In these cases, grief is mixed with anger, guilt, or shame. Spirit often shows up with deep insight and, sometimes, regret. They may not ask for forgiveness. They may simply offer context. A glimpse into their emotional state. A recognition of the pain they caused. These moments can be difficult. But they can also bring understanding. They allow the client to release what they have carried. To name what was never spoken. To begin the process of letting go.

Grief is also present in the medium.

The work opens their heart to sorrow repeatedly. They must know how to feel without absorbing. They must hold space for others while tending to their own emotional landscape. Many mediums have lost deeply. Their ability to hold grief comes from having walked through it themselves. They do not speak from theory. They speak from the sacred ground of experience. This shared humanity is what makes the connection real.

There is also the collective grief that mediums may feel. The grief of ancestral trauma. The grief of cultural loss. The grief that lives in the land, in forgotten histories, in broken systems. When spirit speaks of these things, the medium becomes a voice for something larger. They name what others have buried. They bring light to what was hidden. They allow grief to rise, not as weakness, but as a call to remembrance.

Grief does not end. It changes. It becomes part of the soul's rhythm. It teaches love in its most honest form. It teaches that we do not grieve what we did not love and that love, once awakened, cannot be undone.

The medium becomes a steward of this truth. They do not seek to take the grief away. They walk beside it. They show that within the grief lives the proof of eternal connection.

In every tear, there is a message. In every ache, there is a memory. In every longing, there is a presence waiting to be felt. Mediumship does not close the wound. It blesses it. It speaks to it. It sits quietly beside it. And in that silence, something opens. Something softens. Something begins to heal.

Grief is not the end of love. It is the shape love takes when it has no place to go. Mediumship gives it a place. It offers a path. A voice. A breath. A return and in that return, both the living and the dead remember who they are.

Reflection Questions: Grief as a Portal

1. How has grief changed me; not just emotionally, but spiritually and energetically?

2. What did grief teach me that joy or peace never could?

3. In my own grieving experiences, did I feel closer or farther away from the spirit world and why?

4. What unspoken or unresolved grief might still be shaping how I receive, interpret, or deliver spirit messages?

5. When I sit with the grief of others, what echoes of my own losses awaken within me?

6. Do I allow grief to move through me fully, or do I try to contain or intellectualise it to stay in control?

7. What healing or awakening has come to me only because I allowed myself to grieve deeply?

8. In what ways has grief acted as a spiritual teacher, stripping away illusions and bringing me closer to truth?

9. How does grief shape my mediumship, my empathy, and my ability to hold space with compassion?

10. If I saw grief not as something to survive, but as a sacred initiation, how would that change how I honour it within myself and others?

8. Spirit as Therapist

The role of a medium is often perceived as a simple act of translation, a person stands between the living and the dead, interpreting the messages of those who have crossed over. But in truth, the work is far more intricate.

As any experienced medium will tell you, the spirit world does not only bring forward memories or validations. It often brings healing. And not just emotional comfort, but profound psychological insight. The spirit becomes more than a messenger. The spirit becomes a therapist.

This idea may seem unusual at first. How can a person who has passed on function as a therapist? How can someone who once struggled in life bring healing from beyond it?

The answer lies in the transformation that often occurs after death. Freed from the weight of ego, time, and limitation, many spirits return with a wider perspective. They see with clarity the patterns they could not break while alive. They understand the impact of their actions, the depth of their silence, the way their absence shaped those they left behind. And in this space of awareness, they often return not to take, but to give. They return not to be understood, but to help the living understand themselves.

In a mediumship session, this is felt in the quality of the message. The spirit does not simply say "I love you." They say, "I see you." They say, "I understand now what I could not understand then." They may recall moments of emotional distance, moments when they failed to express care or protection, and speak with remorse and insight.

They acknowledge the client's pain. They affirm the feelings that were dismissed. They name the truth that was never spoken aloud. These moments are not rehearsed. They come through the channel of spirit, often catching even the medium by surprise.

Clients are often stunned by the emotional depth of these exchanges. A father who never said "I am proud of you" in life now expresses it with softness and sincerity. A mother who was cold and unavailable comes through with recognition of how she abandoned her daughter emotionally. A sibling who mocked and belittled finally speaks words of regret.

These are not performances. They are acts of soul-level repair. And the client, hearing these words for the first time, often breaks open. Not in pain, but in release. The inner child within them finally receives what it longed for. And that moment becomes a turning point in their healing journey.

In these readings, the medium is not the therapist. The medium is the conduit through which the therapist speaks. But the healing is very real. The spirit often acts like a therapist because they now see the emotional map of the family line. They know where the fractures occurred. They know what was passed down. They know what was hidden, denied, or minimized and they often seek to interrupt those patterns.

A grandparent may speak to the client not about their own life, but about how the trauma they carried is now affecting their grandchild.

A deceased parent may ask the client to stop the cycle of emotional neglect they inherited. A child may encourage the client to finally seek the help they have avoided. These are not random insights. They are invitations to growth.

Mediumship becomes a form of family therapy, one that transcends generations and reclaims truths that were buried. Many spirits return to explain themselves, not to excuse, but to provide context. A man who was emotionally distant may reveal his own childhood trauma. A woman who was controlling may speak about the fear that shaped her parenting.

These revelations allow the client to understand their story in a new way. They do not erase the pain, but they offer a broader lens. They allow compassion to enter the room. And often, it is this compassion that begins to untangle the emotional knots held within the client's body.

Not all spirits come with wisdom. Some come still wounded, still unsure, still seeking. But even in this state, they often catalyse healing. A spirit who cannot speak becomes a symbol of the family's silence. A spirit who refuses to take responsibility mirrors the resistance the client has felt from others in life.

In this case, the medium must be careful. They must hold both truth and protection. They must honour the spirit's presence without enabling harm. They may gently name the emotional dynamic, offering the client a chance to respond, to speak their own truth, to close the chapter that never found resolution.

There is a sacred intelligence to the timing of these sessions. Spirit often waits until the client is ready. A mother who died ten years ago may come forward only now, because her daughter has finally reached a place of emotional safety. A father may delay his apology until the son has become a father himself and can hear it.

The medium must learn to trust this timing. They do not summon the dead. They invite the possibility and when the time is right, spirit steps through, not just to say hello, but to hold up a mirror.

Some of the most profound spirit messages are not about the past, but about the present emotional state of the client. The spirit sees the depression the client cannot name. They feel the anxiety hiding behind the smile. They know about the choices being made from fear, not truth and they speak to it, not with judgment, but with tenderness.

They remind the client of their strength, their beauty, their worth. They challenge the lie that they are alone. And for many, this is more therapeutic than years of counselling. Not because it replaces therapy, but because it opens the door to it.

Mediums often walk a delicate line in these sessions. They are not licensed therapists, but they are stewards of deep emotional work. They must be grounded, aware, and humble. They must know when to refer a client to professional support.

They must know when the pain being expressed is too complex to hold alone. But they must also honour the healing that does occur in the presence of spirit.

Because some wounds are not psychological. They are soul wounds. And those wounds often require soul-level response.

Spirit does not always heal through words. Sometimes, their presence alone is healing. A person who died suddenly and violently may come through with a calm that surprises the client. They bring peace to the moment of death. They remove the haunting image. They bring light into the place that felt dark and terrifying.

The client's nervous system responds. The fear begins to dissolve. The trauma memory begins to soften. This is not placebo. It is real. The medium has not only delivered a message. They have helped rewire the story of death in the client's mind.

There are also times when spirit acts as a therapist not to the client, but to the medium. During private moments, in dreams, in meditation, or during particularly challenging sessions, the medium may receive insight from their own guides or loved ones. These messages are not always easy. They may challenge the medium's ego. They may reveal blind spots. They may offer wisdom the medium does not want to hear.

But they are always given with love. The spirit world is invested in the growth of the medium, not just their accuracy. Because a clearer channel brings more healing. And a more healed medium becomes a truer vessel.

This co-healing dynamic is one of the most beautiful aspects of the work. Spirit teaches the medium even as the medium delivers the message. Every session becomes an exchange. The medium grows in wisdom, in empathy, in understanding. They become more attuned to the complexity of human emotion. They learn to listen with their whole body, their whole heart and in doing so, they become not just a deliverer of words, but a witness to transformation.

The presence of spirit in the role of therapist also challenges our understanding of what it means to be healed. In the physical world, healing is often equated with curing. But in the spirit world, healing means remembering. It means returning to the truth of who we are. It means releasing shame, dissolving illusions, reclaiming worth.

Spirit does not promise that life will become easy. They promise that we are never alone. They promise that the love we shared was real. That the pain mattered. That the journey continues.

For clients who carry complex grief or trauma, the presence of a spirit therapist can be life changing. It does not replace the need for professional help, but it opens a door. It creates safety. It allows the client to begin to speak what they have never said. And sometimes, that is all that is needed. To be seen. To be heard. To be validated not only by a stranger, but by the very soul they thought had forgotten them.

Spirit as therapist is not a metaphor. It is a lived reality in the work of mediumship. It requires the medium to listen deeply, speak truthfully, and hold space courageously.

It requires humility. It requires reverence. It requires the understanding that every message, every sensation, every emotion is part of a sacred process.

The medium becomes a vessel for healing that transcends time, transcends psychology, and reaches into the soul.

When spirit steps forward to offer guidance, when they name the wound, when they speak to the part of the client that has remained hidden, they are not ghostly echoes. They are living presences in a different form. They are teachers. They are guides. They are therapists of the soul.

And in that moment of sacred exchange, the room becomes quiet. The client's eyes fill with tears. The medium's voice softens. And the spirit, once flesh and now light, holds them both in a space that is outside of time. In that space, something old is released. Something true is spoken. And something deeply human is healed.

Reflection Questions: Spirit as Therapist

1. Have I ever received a message from spirit that felt more healing than anything another human could have offered?

2. In what ways do the spirits I connect with mirror the emotional needs or wounds I am still working through?

3. When I serve as a medium, do I witness spirit acting as a therapist, bringing closure, accountability, or emotional insight?

4. How do I differentiate between spirit guidance and my own projections or personal hopes during a reading?

5. Do I allow the messages from spirit to counsel me as well, or do I only see them as something to deliver to others?

6. What have I learned about emotional resilience, forgiveness, or self-worth through the words of those in spirit?

7. Have I ever felt spirit holding space for me in a moment of grief, fear, or transformation? What did that feel like?

8. In what ways does spirit honour the emotional complexity of the people they once were and what does that teach me about compassion?

9. How do I emotionally process the intimate or painful stories spirit often brings through in sessions?

10. Can I accept that sometimes spirit brings forward not just comfort, but truth that challenges or awakens me?

11. In my own healing journey, have I allowed spirit to walk beside me, or do I only invite them in when I am serving others?

12. If I saw mediumship as not just communication, but co-healing, where spirit and sitter both receive, how would that reshape the way I work

9. The Inner Child in Mediumship

At the heart of every human being lives a younger version of themselves. This inner child is not a metaphor. It is an emotional truth. It is the part of us that first learned how to love, how to fear, how to seek comfort, how to protect ourselves. The inner child is the soul's earliest emotional memory, and whether it was nurtured or neglected, it never disappears. It simply waits beneath the surface of adulthood, behind the masks we wear, inside the decisions we make and the relationships we choose.

The work of mediumship often touches this hidden place. Spirit does not just speak to the adult sitting before the medium. Spirit speaks directly to the child within.

Mediumship is not a clinical process. It is deeply emotional. It requires the medium to feel, to sense, to interpret what is being communicated in both seen and unseen ways.

In many readings, what the spirit is trying to reach is not the logical mind of the client - It is the unspoken longing of the inner child. The one who still hopes to hear "I am proud of you" from a father. The one who still aches to be held by a mother who was never emotionally present. The one who still wonders if they were truly loved. These questions do not always form into words. They live as energy and the medium becomes the voice that finally brings those energies into the light.

In the presence of a medium, the client may not realize that their emotions are not just present grief. They may be experiencing childhood sorrow that has remained unhealed. A father passes away, and suddenly the client finds themselves in tears, not only because he is gone, but because of everything he never said. A mother comes through in spirit, and the client is overwhelmed, not with joy, but with confusion, anger, or a desire for closure that was never given.

These are not uncommon reactions. They are sacred. They are the echoes of the inner child being activated by the presence of a soul that shaped their earliest experiences of love, safety, and belonging.

The spirit world understands the inner child. Spirit sees us in our wholeness, which includes all ages, all memories, all versions of who we have been. A departed parent does not just speak to the adult client. They often address the child they remember. They may reference a toy, a pet, a favourite bedtime story. They may recall a moment that seemed small but meant everything. When this happens, it is not for show. It is for healing. It is to remind the client that they were seen and that their experience was real, that their emotional truth mattered.

For clients who experienced childhood trauma, mediumship can be both cathartic and challenging. A spirit who was abusive or neglectful may come forward. In these cases, the medium must walk with great care. The goal is never to force reconciliation. The goal is to hold space for emotional truth. Sometimes the spirit offers remorse. Sometimes they simply acknowledge their own inability to love. The medium is not there to heal the client directly.

They are there to offer a message that may allow the client to begin their own healing. For the inner child, just hearing the words "I am sorry" or "It was not your fault" can shift years of internalized pain.

Not all inner children are wounded. Some are simply forgotten. Life has taught many people to grow up too quickly, to suppress their joy, to mute their imagination, to stop believing in magic or spirit.

Mediumship often reignites the wonder of the inner child. When a spirit brings forward a childhood memory, a favourite song, or a silly shared joke, the client often laughs through their tears.

It is a moment of reunion not only with their loved one, but with a part of themselves they left behind. That reunion is healing. It allows the soul to expand again, to breathe, to remember that love and play are part of the sacred, not separate from it.

The medium also carries an inner child. The way they receive, interpret, and deliver messages is often influenced by how safe their own inner child feels.

A medium who has been wounded may find themselves triggered during certain readings. A spirit who reminds them of a hurtful parent may cause them to shut down or misinterpret. A child spirit may stir grief the medium has not yet processed. This is why inner child work is essential for those who walk the path of mediumship. The clearer the relationship with one's own inner child, the clearer the channel becomes.

Inner child healing for the medium involves listening to their own emotions, allowing play and creativity, setting boundaries, and honouring the body. It involves noticing when fear arises and asking, "Whose fear is this?" It involves holding space for the part of themselves that still seeks safety and validation.

When the medium tends to this relationship, their sessions become more grounded, more compassionate, and more emotionally balanced. They can hold the grief of others without losing themselves. They can deliver challenging messages with empathy rather than projection.

The spirit world often communicates with the inner child of the client in symbolic ways. A departed grandparent may show up as a protective presence, bringing comfort and guidance. A sibling who died young may come through to say, "I am still with you. You are not alone." A parent may offer the words they never said or revisit a moment the client had forgotten but never healed. These messages often bypass the intellectual mind and land directly in the heart. The client may not be able to explain why they are crying. They simply feel something inside them soften, break open, or finally let go.

Mediumship becomes a place where reparenting begins. The spirit offers what the client never received, not to erase the past, but to heal its residue. The client hears the words they longed for. They feel the presence they missed. And the adult part of them begins to comfort the inner child within. This integration is powerful. It allows the client to move forward with more wholeness, more emotional clarity, more capacity to give and receive love.

Sometimes, the client is invited to speak to their loved one as the child they once were. The medium may say, "If there is anything you have always wanted to say, you can say it now." This invitation often brings emotion to the surface. The client may say, "I needed you and you were not there." Or "I love you and I miss you every day." These expressions are not for the medium. They are for the child who waited a lifetime to be heard. And when the spirit receives those words, and responds with love, the healing is mutual.

Mediumship is not about erasing pain. It is about acknowledging it. It is about bringing light into the places that were hidden. The inner child does not need to be fixed. It needs to be seen. When spirit speaks directly to the child within the client, something profound occurs. The emotional landscape shifts. The old stories lose their grip. The client begins to rewrite their understanding of who they are, not just through the lens of suffering, but through the truth of enduring love.

Children in spirit also communicate through mediumship. These readings are sacred and must be approached with tenderness and humility. The soul of a child who has passed often brings with them joy, innocence, and wisdom beyond their years. They communicate through feeling, through images, through the simplest words. "I am happy," they might say. "I am safe."

They often show the medium their favourite toys, songs, or the way they would cuddle. For grieving parents, these messages are both heartbreaking and healing. The connection reminds them that their child still exists, that their bond is not broken, and that they are still parenting their child through love and memory.

The inner child of the grieving parent often responds to the child in spirit. In those moments, something ancient is healed. Not only is the parent grieving the loss of their child, but also the part of themselves that never fully grew up. Spirit creates space for these layers to meet. The reading becomes more than a message. It becomes a reunion of soul parts, across time and form.

In some readings, the medium may encounter a spirit who died as a child but has matured in the spirit world. These souls often return as guides, bringing insight and strength. They still hold the essence of their childhood personality, but they also carry wisdom. They remind the client that growth continues beyond the body. That the soul does not remain frozen in the moment of death. That life continues in ways the human mind cannot fully understand, but the heart can feel.

The inner child is not a weakness. It is the key to authenticity, creativity, and spiritual connection. Mediumship that honours the inner child becomes more than a communication tool. It becomes a portal to self-understanding.

The messages go deeper. They speak not only to the present, but to the very foundation of who the client believes themselves to be. The spirit world knows how to find this foundation. It knows how to build upon it.

And the medium, as the bridge, learns how to speak with gentleness and strength at the same time.

As we grow older, the voice of the inner child is often drowned out by responsibility, disappointment, and fear. But in the sacred space of mediumship, that voice is heard again. It says, "I remember you." It says, "I still believe in love." It says, "Please do not forget me." Spirit answers that voice with kindness. The medium gives it form. And the client, for a moment, becomes whole again.

Mediumship is the art of remembering. Not just the memories of the dead, but the forgotten truths within the living. The inner child holds many of those truths. When spirit speaks to that part of us, healing is not just possible. It is inevitable. Because in that moment, we remember that we were never truly abandoned. That we were always loved. That within us still lives the wonder, the innocence, and the longing that makes us human and sacred all at once.

Reflection Questions: The Inner Child in Mediumship

1. What was my earliest memory of sensing, seeing, or knowing something others could not and how did the adults around me respond?

2. In what ways does my inner child still long to be seen, believed, or validated for their spiritual gifts?

3. Do I ever feel afraid of being "wrong" or "too much" during a reading and could that fear stem from childhood experiences of rejection or shame?

4. How do I nurture my inner child before and after connecting to spirit? Do I speak to them, comfort them, or include them in the process?

5. What does my inner child believe about safety, sensitivity, and being emotionally open in the world?

6. When I connect with spirit, do I feel playful, curious, or imaginative; qualities of the child self or do I suppress those traits?

7. Has my inner child been wounded by spiritual experiences that were misunderstood, dismissed, or feared by others?

8. What messages from spirit have felt like they were meant more for my inner child than my adult self?

9. How would my mediumship change if I truly allowed my inner child to feel safe, accepted, and supported in my practice?

10. If I asked my inner child what they most want me to remember as a medium, what would they say?

10. Haunted by the Past

There is a common misconception that hauntings only happen in dark, abandoned places. People picture old houses with creaking floorboards, flickering lights, and cold spots in forgotten corners. But the truth is that hauntings are not always physical. They are emotional. They are psychological. They are spiritual imprints left behind not only in places, but in people. The past does not always rest in peace. It lingers, not just in the buildings we fear, but in the body, in the memory, in the family line, in the heart.

Mediumship often reveals this truth in ways that challenge our understanding of ghosts. A haunting is not only a spirit looking for release. It is a moment in time that has refused to let go.

The past haunts us in many forms. It shows up in the grief that will not ease, in the guilt that festers, in the dreams we cannot forget. It speaks through the pain we inherit from our ancestors, through the trauma we bury to keep moving forward.

Mediumship brings the past into the light, not to cause fear, but to offer freedom. When a spirit lingers, when their energy remains active in a place or around a person, it is often because something remains unresolved. Something was denied, hidden, silenced, or left incomplete.

The medium does not banish the past. They bring it into sacred conversation.

Many spirits that are described as ghosts are not malicious. They are confused. They are caught in a loop of emotion or memory. They are trying to finish a story that never received its final chapter. This can happen when a person dies suddenly, traumatically, or without closure. It can happen when there is a deep attachment to a place, a person, or a role they once played. These spirits are not evil. They are lost. And the medium becomes the map.

In some readings, the medium may feel a heavy presence that does not speak in full sentences. Instead, it brings sensation, a tightness in the chest, a feeling of sadness, a mental fog. This is the energy of a lingering spirit. They may not know how to communicate clearly, but their need is palpable. They want to be remembered. They want to be understood. They want to be released from the moment they have been stuck inside.

The medium listens not only with their ears, but with their entire body. They allow the presence to speak in the language of emotion.

Some spirits do not haunt places. They haunt people. They remain close to loved ones who are struggling, to those they feel responsible for, to those with whom they had unfinished business. This can be comforting or draining, depending on the energy of the spirit and the emotional state of the living.

Mediumship can clarify this dynamic. A client may feel they cannot move on after a loss. They feel watched, weighed down, or emotionally stagnant. The medium may sense that the spirit is close, trying to help but unintentionally causing more pain. Through the reading, boundaries can be set, messages can be delivered, and both the living and the dead can find peace.

There are also inherited hauntings, ancestral wounds passed down through generations. These are not caused by an individual ghost, but by collective pain that was never addressed. Abuse, addiction, war, betrayal, abandonment, these leave spiritual residues. Families carry them in their dynamics, their fears, their patterns.

Mediumship often uncovers these themes. A spirit may come forward not to talk about their own life, but to speak about what they were carrying from their parents and grandparents. They show the lineage of pain. They reveal the origin. And they often ask the client to be the one who breaks the cycle.

These ancestral hauntings are not curses in the traditional sense. They are memories that need to be honoured. They are emotions that need to be released. The medium becomes the storyteller, the witness, the one who helps the family remember what was lost or denied. Sometimes this means naming what was hidden. Sometimes it means speaking aloud a name that was never mentioned again. Sometimes it means creating a ritual of remembrance. Through these acts, the haunting begins to lift. The energy of the past is not erased, but it is no longer stuck. It begins to move again.

Mediums also encounter environmental hauntings; places where strong emotions were imprinted into the land or the walls. Hospitals, battlefields, prisons, homes where trauma occurred. These locations often hold residual energy that is not a conscious spirit, but a replay of past events.

The medium feels it as a heaviness or distortion in the atmosphere. It is not interactive, but it is present. These hauntings are like emotional scars on the earth. They speak to the need for healing not just of people, but of places.

In some cases, the medium may be called to perform a clearing or blessing. This is not about force. It is about compassion. The spirit is invited to speak, to share, to be acknowledged. The medium may light candles, say prayers, use herbs or sound.

These tools are not for show. They are sacred technologies that help create safety and openness. The spirit is not cast out. It is guided home. The space is not dominated. It is healed.

There are times when the haunting is within the client's own energy. They are holding onto the past so tightly that it has become a part of their identity. A spirit may point this out, gently reminding the client that they are more than their pain. That they are allowed to live. That letting go does not mean forgetting. The reading becomes an invitation.

The medium may say, "They are asking you to live now." Or "They want you to write the next chapter." These messages can be difficult to hear, but they are sacred. They are the permission the client did not know they needed.

Mediumship also reveals that we are haunted not only by the dead, but by our own unspoken truths.

The spirit comes through, not to deliver facts, but to stir remembrance. The client realizes what they never said. What they never allowed themselves to feel. The haunting lifts when the truth is spoken.

When the client allows themselves to grieve, to forgive, to release. The spirit acts as a mirror. They reflect the parts of the client that are still waiting to be healed.

Not all hauntings are painful. Some are acts of devotion. A spirit remains close out of love, not fear. They walk beside the living, not because they are trapped, but because they choose to remain as protectors or guides. These presences feel light, warm, reassuring. They do not drain energy. They uplift it.

The medium distinguishes this by the way the spirit feels. Heavy spirits feel stagnant. Loving spirits feel expansive. Both may need to be addressed, but in different ways. The medium offers clarity. They help the client understand who is present and why.

When a spirit is truly stuck, the medium may sense disorientation or confusion. These are the spirits who may not realize they have passed, or who are clinging to a specific moment or trauma.

The medium becomes the one who gently informs them, who speaks to them like a friend, not a priest. "You are safe now," they may say. "It is time to let go." These words, simple as they are, can bring immense peace. The spirit begins to move. The energy shifts. The haunting begins to end.

Mediums are not exorcists. They are not here to fight the dead. They are here to listen. To understand. To create bridges. When this is done with compassion and skill, even the most intense hauntings can be transformed. What was once terrifying becomes sacred. What was once confusing becomes clear. What was once heavy becomes light.

The past does not want to hurt us. It wants to be healed. Spirit does not haunt to harm. Spirit remains to be remembered. When we give voice to the stories that were buried, when we feel the emotions that were denied, when we honour the pain instead of fearing it, we open a door to freedom. The medium is the one who walks with us to that door. And on the other side is peace.

We are all haunted by something. A memory, a regret, a name we dare not say. But when we face it, when we invite it into conversation, it changes. Mediumship is the sacred art of that conversation. It is the space where the past is not erased, but integrated. Where the dead are not feared but understood. Where the living are no longer alone in their pain. To be haunted is to be human. To listen to the haunting is to be brave. And to allow that haunting to become a healing is to become whole.

The past can become a haunting presence when pain, regret, or trauma remain unresolved, looping in the mind like echoes in an abandoned hall. To help someone move beyond this, the first step is to gently bring awareness to the grip the past still holds. Encourage them to name what happened, not to relive it, but to acknowledge it with truth and compassion. Validation is crucial, many wounds deepen in silence.

Offer a space where their story can be held without judgment, reminding them they are not what happened to them. Guide them to see the difference between remembering and identifying with the past. Healing begins not by forgetting, but by choosing to no longer let it define the present.

Next, help them build a sense of safety in the now. This may include grounding exercises, energy work, journaling, or daily rituals that remind the soul it is no longer in danger. Introduce the concept of spiritual alchemy, the idea that pain can become purpose, and that their story can transform from an anchor to a doorway. Encourage forgiveness, not for the sake of others, but as a release for the self. Most importantly, remind them they have the right to create a new narrative. They are not broken but becoming. The past shaped them, yes - but the present moment is where they begin to write something different.

Reflection Questions: Haunted by the Past

1. What moments or memories from my past still carry an emotional charge when I think of them and how might they affect my connection to spirit?

2. Are there people, places, or situations I avoid because of what they trigger in me, and could those be connected to unfinished energetic stories?

3. Have I ever felt that something I carry such as fear, grief, shame, did not begin with me? Could it belong to an ancestor or a past life?

4. In what ways do my own unresolved wounds shape the types of spirits, messages, or emotional themes that appear in my readings?

5. Have I ever experienced a reading that unexpectedly brought up my own pain and how did I respond to it?

6. What patterns continue to repeat in my life or in my mediumship work that may be echoes of unhealed past events?

7. Do I feel haunted more by people or by feelings and what is the deeper truth beneath that haunting?

8. What part of my past have I tried to spiritually bypass rather than truly integrate and heal?

9. If I could sit with the younger version of myself or a past life self who still feels "stuck," what would I say to them?

10. What am I finally ready to release, not just from memory, but from my energy body and spiritual path?

11. The Wounded Medium

There is a quiet truth that we rarely speak aloud in the world of spiritual service. It is this: the medium is often wounded. Behind the serene presence, the accurate messages, and the sacred work of connecting the living and the dead, there is a human being who has suffered deeply.

The path of the medium is rarely one of ease or untouched light. It is often marked by trauma, by loss, by emotional isolation, and a sensitivity that was once unbearable. Before the medium becomes a bridge for others, they must first cross the terrain of their own sorrow, and it is precisely because of this journey through pain that they become capable of holding space for others.

The medium is not a distant oracle. The medium is a witness. The medium is a survivor.

The archetype of the wounded healer is ancient. In myth, story, and spiritual tradition, the healer does not emerge from comfort but from suffering. The shaman falls ill and journeys into the otherworld to understand their pain. The mystic is broken open by grief and becomes a vessel for divine love. The priestess loses everything and learns to speak with the ancestors.

In every tradition, the one who sees into the hidden realms must first be brought to the edge of their own endurance. This is not cruelty. It is preparation. The soul of the medium is stretched and shaped by their suffering so that they might one day become a container for the healing of others.

Many mediums report that their abilities first began to emerge after a personal crisis. A loss that shattered their world. An illness that left them on the threshold between life and death. A childhood marked by emotional neglect or abuse. A sense of not belonging, not being understood, not being safe in the world.

These experiences are not coincidences. They are initiations. They open the psychic senses because they break down the walls of the ordinary. When the world no longer makes sense, when the systems of control collapse, the soul reaches out in new directions.

The medium becomes sensitive not as a choice, but as a response. The pain tears away the illusion and leaves the spirit exposed. And in that exposure, the voices of the unseen begin to speak.

But this sensitivity is not easy to live with. The wounded medium does not simply wake up one day enlightened. They must learn to live with their sensitivity, to navigate a world that often feels too loud, too fast, too sharp. They may feel everything. They may struggle to know which emotions are theirs and which belong to others. They may absorb the energy of a room, of a person, of a place.

They may be dismissed as dramatic, unstable, or too emotional and if they were never taught to understand this sensitivity, they may believe these judgments.

They may internalize the idea that something is wrong with them. They may learn to hide what they feel, to disconnect, to numb. But beneath the surface, the soul still listens. The spirit world still calls.

It is common for wounded mediums to try to live ordinary lives. To follow the rules. To fit in. To suppress what they know and feel. But eventually, the pressure becomes too great. The soul refuses to remain silent. The dreams become more vivid. The synchronicities more obvious. The longing more intense. The pain, when not expressed, becomes physical.

The medium begins to feel ill without cause, exhausted without reason, anxious without context. This is not dysfunction. This is the soul knocking on the door of awareness. The spirit world does not force itself upon the medium. But it does wait. It waits for the moment when the medium can no longer deny who they are.

The moment of awakening for the wounded medium is often tender and terrifying. It may come through a reading, a vision, a voice, a dream, or a sudden knowing. It may arrive with awe or with fear. But however it comes, it is a return. A return to the truth that was always there.

The medium remembers that they have always felt different, always sensed more, always known there was something beyond. This memory does not erase the wounds. It brings them into the light. The medium sees how their pain has shaped their gift. How their empathy was born from abandonment. How their insight was forged in silence. How their ability to feel for others came from not being felt themselves.

The process of becoming a medium is not just about opening psychic senses. It is about healing. The wounded medium must learn to sit with their own grief, not only the grief of others. They must face the trauma they have carried, the beliefs they have inherited, the patterns that have kept them in fear.

They must learn to tell the truth about their own story. Because if they do not, those wounds will speak through the messages they deliver. They will project instead of perceive. They will comfort instead of confront. They will read from their pain instead of their presence. And while this does not make them fraudulent, it does limit the depth and clarity of their work.

Healing as a medium is not a destination. It is a way of life. It means returning again and again to the parts of the self that have been hidden, denied, or shamed. It means creating rituals for release, for integration, for grounding. It means having the courage to receive what spirit offers not only for the client, but for the self.

It means having boundaries, not walls. Compassion, not saviour complexes. Humility, not false modesty and most of all, it means remembering that mediumship is not a performance. It is a relationship.

The wounded medium often struggles with self-worth. They may doubt their ability, their right to serve, their value as a messenger. They may feel unworthy of the praise they receive or terrified of criticism. These fears are not signs of failure.

They are signs of tenderness. The heart that has been wounded does not forget easily. It takes time to learn that you are safe. That you are not broken. That your sensitivity is not a curse, but a compass. The medium who learns to trust themselves learns to trust spirit more fully. The channel becomes clearer. The messages become more precise. And the presence they offer becomes more healing.

One of the greatest gifts the wounded medium can offer is presence without judgment. Because they have known pain, they can sit with pain. Because they have faced their own darkness, they do not flinch when others do. Because they have walked through grief, they know how to hold the hand of the grieving.

This is not something that can be taught in a workshop. It is learned through living. Through breaking and mending. Through silence and prayer. Through trial and error. Through a thousand moments of listening to the still small voice within and choosing to follow it.

The wounded medium also learns discernment. They know what it feels like to be overwhelmed, to be taken advantage of, to be drained. They learn to say no, not from hardness, but from wisdom. They learn to protect their energy not from fear, but from respect. They know that healing others does not mean sacrificing themselves. They know that spirit does not ask them to suffer endlessly. They understand that the wound is a beginning, not a destiny. It is what opened the door. But it is not the home.

Some mediums will continue to carry pain. The wound may never fully disappear. But it transforms. It softens. It becomes less of a sharp edge and more of a quiet companion. The medium no longer lives in the wound. They live in the wisdom the wound created. They carry it with reverence. They speak from it with truth. They use it not to define themselves, but to understand others. This is what makes their presence healing. Not perfection, but authenticity.

The clients who come to the wounded medium often sense this. They may not know the medium's story, but they feel the depth. They feel safe to cry, to confess, to grieve. They feel met, not analysed. They feel held, not fixed. This is the medicine the wounded medium offers. Not answers, but presence. Not authority, but companionship. Not certainty, but trust.

In the sacred work of mediumship, the most important relationship is not only between the medium and the spirit, but between the medium and themselves. Every reading is an echo of that relationship. Every message passes through the lens of the medium's heart. The clearer, kinder, and more healed that heart is, the more potent the message becomes, and this is not about being perfect. It is about being real.

The wounded medium does not hide their story. They honour it. They understand that their sensitivity is not something to be overcome, but something to be embraced.

They know that the tears they shed are not weakness, but devotion. That the fear they feel before a powerful reading is not doubt, but reverence. That the exhaustion that follows deep work is not failure, but evidence of care.

Mediums who embrace their wounds become lighthouses for others. They do not lead by claiming to know everything. They lead by being willing to feel. To stand in the storm and still be grounded. To speak the truth even when it shakes. To listen to the whisper of spirit even when their own heart is breaking. These are the mediums who change lives. Not because they are famous or flawless, but because they are willing to be human.

In the end, it is not the absence of wounds that makes a medium powerful. It is the way they have transformed those wounds into wisdom. It is the way they have turned pain into presence, sorrow into strength, silence into speech. The wounded medium does not claim to save others. They walk beside them. They share what they have learned. They offer their presence as a reminder that healing is possible, that love never dies, and that even the deepest wound can become a sacred doorway.

Reflection Questions: The Wounded Medium

1. What emotional wounds do I carry that still whisper through my mediumship, whether in fear, insecurity, or over-giving?

2. In what ways has my pain sharpened my sensitivity and in what ways has it made me feel unsafe in my gift?

3. Do I feel the need to prove myself in readings, and could that be a reflection of where I still feel unworthy or unseen?

4. How do I hold space for others when I am still healing parts of myself and what boundaries or rituals help me protect that space?

5. What parts of my life story do I avoid revisiting, even though they continue to live quietly in the background of my work?

6. When I feel drained, disconnected, or overly emotional after a reading, is it spirit or my wounds being triggered?

7. Have I ever used my mediumship to feel needed, validated, or important? And what would it mean to let that go?

8. What would change in my mediumship if I fully accepted my wounds not as flaws, but as sacred initiations into deeper empathy?

12. Dissociation or Divine?

There is a mysterious and often misunderstood intersection between psychological defence and spiritual perception. In the world of psychology, dissociation is seen as a coping mechanism, a way the mind protects itself from overwhelming stress, trauma, or emotional pain by creating a sense of detachment.

In the world of spiritual experience, however, there exists something remarkably similar in appearance but vastly different in origin and purpose. A state of expanded consciousness in which the soul reaches beyond the body to connect with the divine, the unseen, and the eternal.

For mediums, the boundary between dissociation and divine connection can be delicate and complex. It is not uncommon for a medium to have a history of dissociative tendencies, not because they are mentally unstable, but because their soul learned early on how to navigate between worlds as a matter of survival. The very ability that once protected them becomes, later in life, the gateway through which they connect to spirit, other realms and dimensions and is very real for the authentic conduit.

To understand this, we must first explore what dissociation truly is.

In psychological terms, dissociation involves a disruption in the normal integration of consciousness, memory, identity, emotion, perception, and even bodily awareness. Dissociation ranges from mild daydreaming or zoning out to more intense experiences such as depersonalization, derealization, or dissociative amnesia and disorders.

For someone who has experienced trauma, especially in childhood, dissociation often becomes a learned response. When the body cannot escape a threat and the mind cannot emotionally process it, the soul steps out. It detaches. It observes from a distance. It waits for safety in another conscious state of mind.

Over time, this becomes an unconscious habit. The child who once had to leave their body in order to survive a threatening situation, becomes the adult who still unconsciously steps out when the perceived situation they are in feel too intense.

Now consider the experience of spirit communication. The medium often enters a state of heightened awareness, leaving behind the chatter of the thinking mind, entering a stillness where impressions come through, voices whisper, images form, and emotions arise that do not belong to them. They may feel outside of time. They may lose track of their own body. They may speak words they do not understand until after they have left their lips.

The question is; could this be dissociation or is it divine communion? Or is it both?

For many mediums, the answer resides in awareness. The difference between dissociation and divine connection is not only about symptoms or experiences. It is about intention, embodiment, and the presence of safety. Dissociation pulls us out of our bodies because we are afraid and disconnects us from ourselves in order to protect us from any trauma or pain we could potentially be sensing.

Divine connection, by contrast, invites us to expand beyond our bodies while staying grounded in love and reality. Divine connection is not an escape. It is a consciousness of spiritual connection beyond the earthly realm while staying mindfully present.

The pathways to both states can feel the same. Many mediums, especially those with complex trauma histories, healed or unhealed, have to relearn what it means to be present in their body while still receiving the connection from spirit. They have to explore and know the difference between disassociation and awakening. This takes time. It takes therapy, reflection, and a willingness to sit within the discomfort.

The medium learns to ask, "Am I checking out or am I tuning in?" They notice the subtle differences. When they are dissociating, they may feel fragmented, ungrounded, foggy, or detached. When they are in connection with spirit, they may feel awake, alert, peaceful, and clear.

Dissociation is a survival strategy, often unconscious. It creates a split between the emotional body and the thinking mind. In contrast, divine connection is a spiritual conscious practice of surrendering to the unknown with full awareness without fear.

The medium who works with intention, groundedness, and care can begin to transform the very pathways that were once used for escape into highways for connection. The same sensitivity that once led to fragmentation becomes the channel through which spirit flows.

This is not to pathologize the medium's experience. Rather, it is to acknowledge the psychological reality behind many intuitive awakenings. It is to honour the full human experience, recognizing that spiritual gifts often arise from the places we were once broken. The wounded child who left their body during trauma may grow into the adult who now receives messages from the beyond. The fear that once caused shutdown is now the door through which healing light enters.

It is also important to understand that many spiritual states can mimic dissociative symptoms. When a medium enters a trance state, they may have difficulty remembering what was said. When they experience deep connection to spirit, they may feel less attached to the material world.

They may speak of timelessness, of visions, of sudden insights that feel more real than their physical surroundings. These experiences are not inherently unhealthy. But they must be integrated. The medium must return to the body, to the present, to their breath. Grounding becomes not only a spiritual practice, but a psychological necessity.

This is why many mediums are drawn to body-based practices like yoga, tai chi, dance, or somatic healing. These practices help create a healthy bridge between spirit and self. They allow the medium to feel safe in their body so that they do not need to leave it in order to connect.

In fact, the more grounded the medium becomes, the clearer the messages. Spirit does not require suffering to speak. It requires presence.

The language of spirit is subtle. It often arrives in the same ways trauma once did—through sensation, feeling, imagery, and intuition. The body that once trembled in fear now trembles in recognition. The heart that once broke with grief now opens with love. The difference is not the form, but the context. Spirit speaks in waves of emotion because emotion is the most direct pathway to the soul.

The medium, in healing their own emotional body, becomes more able to translate these waves with compassion and discernment.

There is also a spiritual humility that comes with acknowledging the overlap between dissociation and divine connection. The medium learns not to assume every sensation is a message. They learn to check in with themselves first. They learn to ask, "Is this mine? Is this trauma, or is this truth?" They learn to differentiate between intuition and fear, between anxiety and urgency, between the voice of the wounded self and the voice of spirit. This discernment is not a rejection of spiritual experience. It is what makes the experience trustworthy.

For those who are still healing from dissociation, the practice of mediumship must be approached gently. Spirit will not ask the medium to bypass their healing. In fact, the more the medium resists their own emotional work, the more distorted the messages can become.

The spirit world is compassionate, but it also reflects what is within. A fragmented channel often receives fragmented impressions. A grounded channel becomes a clear and safe bridge.

Mediumship, then, becomes not only a gift, but a healing path. It requires the medium to develop emotional regulation, self-awareness, and nervous system support. It invites the medium to reconnect with their body, their boundaries, their story. It asks the medium to be honest, with themselves, with their pain, with their process and in doing so, it transforms the old pattern of dissociation into a sacred skill of communion.

There is also an element of mystery that must be respected. Not every spiritual experience can be explained or dissected. Some moments defy psychology and science. Some moments lift us out of ourselves in ways that are profoundly healing. But even in these moments, the body matters.

The heart matters. The integration matters. It is not enough to reach the heavens. We must also learn how to return and live with the message we received.

The question of dissociation versus divine is not one that needs to be answered with certainty. It is a question that invites reflection. It invites the medium to stay curious, to stay present, to stay in relationship with both their humanity and their spirituality.

It reminds us that the path of the medium is not to escape the world, but to be fully in it with eyes open, heart open, and spirit attuned.

There is great beauty in this balance. The medium who can walk between worlds without losing themselves becomes not only a messenger, but a teacher.

They model what it looks like to feel deeply, to connect profoundly, and to return whole. They show that it is possible to be spiritual and embodied, intuitive and self-aware, open and discerning.

The path is not easy. It asks much. But it gives even more. It gives the medium a chance to reclaim their sensitivity as sacred. To rewrite the story of their pain. To stand in the truth of who they are, not as someone who floats above life, but as someone who walks with grace through it.

In the end, the divine is not found in dissociation. It is found in presence. In the courage to stay. In the willingness to feel. In the soft strength of a soul who has returned to their body, their truth, and their calling.

Reflection Questions: Dissociation or Divine

1. When I connect to spirit, do I feel more embodied or less, do I leave my body, or deepen my presence within it?

2. Are there times I've mistaken emotional numbing or disconnection for being in a spiritual "trance" state?

3. How do I know when I am receiving true guidance versus retreating from discomfort through spiritual bypassing?

4. Do I sometimes use my gift to avoid facing unresolved emotional pain or difficult human experiences?

5. What physical sensations or emotional clues tell me when I'm grounded in divine connection versus psychologically escaping?

6. Have I ever felt addicted to spiritual highs or readings as a way to avoid my everyday reality or inner healing?

7. What role does my breath, body awareness, or environment play in keeping me anchored during mediumship work?

8. When spirit is truly present, how does that differ from when I am dissociating or feeling overwhelmed?

9. Am I willing to pause and check in with myself emotionally before, during, and after connecting with spirit?

10. What would it mean to see my body and emotions not as distractions from the divine, but as part of the divine experience?

13. Empathy, Boundaries, and Burnout

Empathy is often celebrated as one of the most beautiful human traits. It allows us to feel what others feel, to understand suffering, to offer comfort without the need for explanation. For mediums, empathy is not just a virtue. It is the very mechanism through which messages are received.

Empathy allows the medium to step into the emotional landscape of another person, to sense the grief of the living and the echoes of the dead. It is the bridge between energy and understanding. Yet what is often not spoken about is the cost of empathy when it is unboundaried.

Empathy without containment becomes enmeshment. Feeling without discernment becomes absorption and over time, this emotional saturation leads to what many authentic mediums quietly suffer through, burnout.

To understand this, we must first recognize the depth of what a medium holds during a session. They are not simply passing along words. They are standing between worlds. They are opening themselves to sorrow, to longing, to trauma, to love so fierce it can break a person open.

They feel the grief of the mother who lost a child, the confusion of the man who lost his partner to suicide, the guilt of the daughter who did not say goodbye. They feel the energy of the spirit who wants to be known, the urgency of the messages trying to come through, the intensity of the emotion that never found voice while the person was alive.

Empathy allows the medium to go that deep. It is a gift that makes their readings feel personal, healing, and unforgettable. But if the medium does not learn how to protect their own energy, that same empathy becomes a wound. It becomes a doorway through which everything enters and nothing exits.

The medium begins to carry the sorrow of every client. They start to feel tired, unmotivated, overwhelmed. They may feel emotional even when alone, drained after a short conversation, or reluctant to sit for another session. These are not just signs of being tired. They are signs of energetic exhaustion.

Burnout does not arrive suddenly. It builds over time. And for mediums, it builds silently, hidden behind their ability to continue showing up.

Boundaries are the medicine. But boundaries are not always easy for highly sensitive or empathic people to implement. The very sensitivity that allows the medium to feel the needs of others can also make them feel guilty for saying no. They may struggle to assert their limits because they do not want to seem cold, selfish, or unavailable.

They may say yes when they mean no, give more than they have, and believe that being of service means being endlessly available.

This is the dangerous narrative of self-sacrifice disguised as spirituality and it must be dismantled.

A boundary is not a wall. It is a threshold. It says, "This is where I end and you begin." It says, "I will meet you with presence, but not at the cost of my own well-being." It is not a rejection of others. It is an affirmation of self.

The most powerful mediums are not the ones who give everything. They are the ones who give with clarity, with sustainability, with intention. They do not serve from depletion. They serve from overflow. And that overflow only exists when they have protected their inner well.

Energetic boundaries begin with awareness. The medium must learn to notice what belongs to them and what does not. This takes practice. At the end of a session, they might ask, "How much of what I am feeling is mine?" If they feel tired, heavy, or emotionally off-balance, it is a sign that they have taken something in that needs to be released.

Grounding exercises, breathwork, visualization, and cleansing rituals are not optional extras. They are essential practices. The medium must clear their field, close the energetic door, and return to their own body fully.

Physical boundaries are just as important. Mediums must learn to schedule time for rest, to say no to additional clients when they are full, and to honour their need for solitude. They must learn to listen to the signals of their body, which often speaks before the mind can. Headaches, stomach aches, chronic fatigue, and insomnia are all signs that the body is carrying too much. These are not flaws. They are messages.

The body is asking for rest, for space, for care. The medium who ignores these signals may find themselves unable to connect, unable to receive clearly, or emotionally reactive in ways they do not understand.

Burnout also manifests emotionally. The medium may begin to feel apathetic. Where once they were moved by the beauty of a reading, now they feel numb. Where once they felt joy in serving others, now they feel burdened. They may begin to dread sessions that used to inspire them. This emotional shutdown is the soul's way of saying, "I need tending too."

The medium must then turn inward. They must ask, "What have I been carrying that is not mine? What part of me have I neglected in service to others? What does my spirit need right now?"

The work of mediumship is sacred. But it is not meant to cost the medium their own well-being. Spirit does not require the medium to suffer. Spirit requires the medium to be present. And presence cannot be faked. It arises from a place of stability, of rest, of internal peace.

The most profound readings come not from a place of emotional fusion, but from a place of embodied compassion. The medium feels deeply, but does not drown. They see clearly, but do not lose themselves in the story.

Empathy, when balanced with boundaries, becomes wisdom. It becomes a tool for connection rather than a cause for depletion. The medium begins to trust that they do not have to feel everything in order to serve. They learn that holding space does not mean absorbing pain. They learn that being a vessel for spirit also means being a steward of their own energy. And in this way, their gift becomes sustainable.

There is also a myth that the more drained a medium feels, the more accurate or spiritual they must be. This martyr complex is deeply ingrained in spiritual communities. It equates burnout with dedication. It confuses exhaustion with evidence of worth. But burnout is not a badge of honour. It is a sign of imbalance. It is a message from the soul that says, "Come back. Rest. Restore."

The medium who listens to this message becomes stronger. The one who ignores it may find their gift beginning to fade.

Rest is not laziness. It is part of the cycle. Just as the earth has seasons, so does the medium. There are times to serve, times to retreat, times to listen, and times to be silent. Honouring this rhythm is part of the spiritual path. It is not always easy. The world may demand more.

Clients may want more. The ego may whisper that rest is failure. But the soul knows better. The soul knows that retreat is renewal. That stillness is power. That silence is the place where the deepest messages are born.

Burnout also affects the clarity of the channel. A tired medium may misinterpret symbols, confuse emotions, or become reactive. Their readings may become more about their own state than the message itself. This is not because they are unskilled. It is because they are depleted.

The solution is not to try harder. It is to pause. To reset. To allow themselves to be held. Mediums need support too. They need spaces where they are not the guide, but the one being guided. They need healing, nourishment, community, and care.

Empathy is sacred. It is the heart of mediumship. But empathy without boundaries is a fire without a container. It burns everything in its path. The medium must learn to build the container. To honour their own emotions. To know when they are full. To recognize when they need to step back. This is not weakness. This is mastery.

The journey of the medium is not just about learning how to connect with spirit. It is about learning how to live in a human body while doing so. It is about learning how to feel deeply and protect that sensitivity. How to listen without absorbing. How to care without collapsing. This is the true work. This is the unseen labour behind every reading. And it deserves respect.

When the medium finds the balance between empathy and boundaries, they become a beacon. Their energy becomes clear, strong, and magnetic. Clients feel safe in their presence. Spirit trusts their channel. And the medium, in turn, feels sustained.

They serve from love, not obligation. They give with joy, not resentment. They speak from fullness, not fatigue.

Empathy, boundaries, and burnout are not side topics. They are central to the life of the medium. They are not issues to be managed. They are invitations to deepen into truth. To honour the self as much as the service. To recognize that the most powerful medium is not the one who gives everything, but the one who knows how to return to themselves again and again.

In this returning, the medium becomes whole. In this wholeness, the messages become clearer. The presence becomes deeper. The work becomes more graceful. And the medium, no longer drowning in empathy or defined by burnout, becomes what they were always meant to be a bridge between worlds, grounded in love, held in truth, and sustained by the very spirit they serve.

Reflection Questions: Empathy, Boundaries, and Burnout

1. Do I know the difference between feeling with someone and taking on their pain as my own and how often do I cross that line?

2. What situations or types of clients leave me feeling energetically drained, and what might that reveal about my boundaries?

3. Have I ever continued to serve or connect when my body or spirit was asking me to rest and what were the consequences?

4. How do I replenish myself after deep emotional or spiritual work, and is that enough?

5. What unspoken beliefs do I carry about being available, selfless, or "on" for others at the expense of myself?

6. In what ways does my empathy feel like a gift and when does it feel like a weight I do not know how to carry?

7. Do I know how to say no with love or do I fear disappointing others more than I honour my own limits?

8. If burnout is a message from my soul, what is it trying to teach me about how I care for myself while caring for others?

9. What daily or weekly practices help me clear, protect, and restore my energy and what am I neglecting that I know I need?

10. How would my mediumship change if I truly believed that preserving my energy is not selfish, but sacred?

14. Collective Trauma, Collective Spirit

There are wounds that do not belong to one person alone. There are sorrows that echo through families, communities, and entire nations. There are memories so painful, so vast, that they become woven into the fabric of culture itself. These are not the private heartbreaks of individuals. They are the griefs of many. We call this collective trauma, and it is carried not only in minds and hearts, but in bodies, in stories, in silences, and in the very air we breathe.

Collective trauma is not just remembered. It is inherited. It lives in the nervous systems of generations. It shapes the choices people make, the beliefs they hold, and the way they experience the world. And for the medium, it becomes part of the unseen field through which spirit speaks.

Mediumship does not exist in a vacuum. It is not a purely personal experience. When a medium opens to the spirit world, they are not only opening to individual spirits. They are stepping into a much larger field of energy, an energetic ecosystem that includes the emotional residues of wars, migrations, famines, genocides, colonization, natural disasters, pandemics, and systemic violence.

The medium is not just a translator of messages from the departed. They become a vessel for the unresolved energy of history. They hear the voices of those who were silenced, feel the pain of those who were erased, and carry the stories that were never allowed to be told.

Collective trauma often enters a reading subtly. The client may come with a personal loss, but as the session unfolds, the medium begins to sense a weight that is much older, much larger, much deeper. It may show up as heaviness in the body, as images from a different time or place, or as emotions that do not match the individual story being shared.

The client may be grieving the loss of a grandparent, but what emerges is the pain of displacement from an ancestral homeland. They may be processing a recent illness, but what surfaces is the memory of a community that was once ravaged by disease and abandonment. The medium may not immediately understand what is happening, but with experience, they begin to recognize the signs of collective grief.

Spirit also speaks from within this collective space. There are ancestors who return not only to bring comfort, but to speak of what they endured. They come from war zones, refugee camps, boarding schools, forced labour camps, and forgotten villages. They come to remember the children who never came home, the languages that were stolen, the ceremonies that were banned. They come not to accuse, but to heal. They come with tears, with songs, with prayers and they ask the living to listen.

When a medium encounters collective trauma, the responsibility shifts. It is no longer just about personal messages. It becomes about witnessing history through the eyes of the soul.

It becomes about validating experiences that were denied, giving voice to pain that was silenced, and offering a sacred space where the invisible becomes known. This is not light work. It requires courage, emotional strength, and a deep respect for cultural context. The medium must understand that they are stepping into sacred ground, into the grief of entire peoples, into the echoes of systemic injustice.

This is where mediumship begins to resemble sacred activism. The medium becomes not just a messenger, but a vessel for truth. They become part of a much-needed process of remembrance. This does not mean taking on the pain of others or claiming stories that are not theirs to hold. It means listening with humility.

It means creating spaces where others can speak. It means acknowledging the ways in which collective trauma affects the present. And it means trusting that spirit does not bring these stories through without purpose. There is always a reason. There is always a healing waiting to happen.

Clients who carry collective trauma often do not know the full extent of what they are carrying. They may feel sadness they cannot explain, anxiety that has no name, or shame that seems to have no origin. They may feel disconnected from their culture, their land, their family. Spirit often steps in to reconnect the threads. A grandmother may show the herbs she used to gather before colonization stripped away the right to practice traditional medicine. A great-grandfather may speak about the language he spoke only in whispers, for fear of punishment.

These messages are not romanticized. They are real. They carry the weight of history. And when delivered with compassion, they allow the client to feel seen in a way they never have before.

Mediums working with collective trauma must educate themselves. This is not just spiritual work. It is social, historical, and cultural. They must learn about the histories of oppression that have shaped the people they serve. They must understand the lasting impact of racism, colonialism, slavery, religious persecution, and systemic violence.

They must examine their own biases and privileges. This is not about shame. It is about awareness. Spirit does not speak in a vacuum, and neither should the medium.

It is also vital for the medium to work in collaboration with other healing professionals.

Collective trauma often requires therapeutic integration. A spirit may bring through a message that touches on abuse, cultural shame, or historical violence. The client may need support beyond the session. The medium must know when to refer, when to pause, and when to simply hold space without trying to fix. This work is delicate. It is sacred and it is often ongoing.

There is also beauty in collective spirit. Just as there is collective trauma, there is also collective resilience, collective love, collective memory. Ancestors come not only to share pain, but to share strength. They bring songs, recipes, dances, rituals, laughter. They bring reminders of who we are beyond the wound.

They speak of survival, of beauty, of the sacred bonds that time and violence could not destroy. They come to say, "You are not alone." They come to say, "You belong." They come to remind us that even in the darkest histories, the light of spirit remains.

Mediumship that touches collective spirit often feels different. It is expansive. It feels like standing in a circle rather than a one-on-one conversation. The messages may be directed to the client, but they carry relevance for many. The spirit may speak of land, of community, of future generations. They may ask for ritual, for ceremony, for reconnection.

These messages are often deeply emotional. They open not just the heart, but the soul. They awaken ancestral memory. They call the client home—not only to their family, but to their spirit line.

Mediums who serve in communities that have experienced deep historical trauma have a sacred role. They must listen more than they speak. They must approach the work with reverence, not ego. They must understand that they are being invited into something larger than themselves. And they must be willing to sit in the discomfort of not knowing. Spirit will guide them. But humility is the key.

Collective trauma also shows up in the land. There are places where grief is embedded in the soil. Places where violence occurred, where ceremonies were interrupted, where communities were broken. The medium may feel this as soon as they enter. The air is heavy. The birds are quiet. The body tenses. The past is alive. Spirit may speak from these places, asking for acknowledgment, for offering, for healing. A candle lit. A song sung. A stone placed. These acts are not performative. They are sacred exchanges. They say, "We remember."

In group readings or circles, collective trauma can rise in surprising ways. One person shares, and suddenly the whole room is crying. A message is given, and many nod in recognition. This is not coincidence. It is the field of collective spirit moving. The medium becomes the facilitator of group healing.

They do not need to analyse or control. They simply create a safe container. The healing happens in the space between the words. In the breath. In the silence. In the tears.

Spirit may also bring through collective visions. Dreams of future peace. Images of reconnection. Guidance for activism, for community building, for reconciliation. These are not fantasies. They are blueprints.

Spirit works not only to heal the past, but to shape the future. The medium, then, becomes a channel not just for remembrance, but for re-creation. They carry the seeds of what could be. They become vision keepers.

There is great responsibility in this. But there is also great reward. To serve the collective spirit is to step into a role that is ancient and needed. It is to become a bridge not only between the living and the dead, but between generations. Between cultures. Between the wound and the healing. Between the past and the potential.

This work cannot be done alone. Mediums must find support, a tribe of friendships. They must care for their bodies, their spirits, their mental health. The weight of collective trauma is too much for one person to carry. But in shared healing, in shared truth, in shared sacredness, it becomes manageable. It becomes transformative.

In the presence of collective spirit, the room becomes sacred, and the air feels full. The ancestors gather. The stories rise.

And the medium, humbled and honoured, becomes the voice that says, "We see you. We remember. We are still here."

Mediumship, at its most profound, is not about proving the afterlife. It is about healing life itself. It is about weaving together the fragmented stories, the forgotten names, the silenced truths. It is about becoming a vessel for remembrance and repair.

When the medium steps into this role with clarity, care, and reverence, they are no longer just a spiritual practitioner. They become part of the living archive of humanity. A keeper of memory. A voice for the many.

And in that sacred exchange, where the pain of the past meets the hope of the present, the medium does not stand alone. They stand with spirit. They stand with the ancestors. They stand with every soul who has waited for their story to be told.

Reflection Questions: Collective Trauma, Collective Spirit

1. In what ways do I carry emotional weight that does not feel entirely mine, could it belong to my culture, ancestry, or the collective?

2. How have global events, collective losses, or ancestral traumas impacted my nervous system, worldview, or sensitivity as a medium?

3. When I connect to spirit, do I ever sense the presence of energies or voices beyond the individual, voices that speak for a people, a history, or a forgotten truth?

4. What parts of my own story are shaped by inherited fear, silence, or survival patterns passed down through generations?

5. How does collective grief show up in my mediumship practice and am I equipped to hold that level of pain with care?

6. Do I feel a responsibility to bear witness to suffering through my work and where must I also protect my own spirit in the process?

7. How do I differentiate between personal emotion and collective emotional energy when I feel overwhelmed or burdened?

8. What role might my mediumship play in healing not just individuals, but the energetic residue of cultural, ancestral, or planetary trauma?

15. When Spirit Brings Abuse to Light

Mediumship is often seen as a source of comfort. It is a sacred bridge between the living and the dead, a space where love is reaffirmed and connection is restored. For many, it is a balm for grief and a light in the darkness. But there are times when spirit does not come with sweetness. There are moments in mediumship when the message is not about fond memories or gentle reassurance. Instead, it is about truth. Unspoken.

Unacknowledged. Sometimes terrifying. Sometimes painful. These are the moments when spirit brings abuse to light. And in these moments, the medium becomes not only a messenger, but a witness to human suffering that has crossed time, space, and death itself.

Spirits do not bring messages of abuse lightly. They do not come to harm or shock. They come because healing is needed. They come because a truth has been buried too long. Because the wound that was hidden has festered in the family line. Because a soul cannot move forward, or a life cannot grow, until the silence is broken.

These are not messages that mediums are trained to deliver in workshops. There is no formula for handling this level of emotional and spiritual intensity. Each experience is different. Each one demands presence, ethics, intuition, and deep compassion.

The first question a medium must ask themselves when abuse arises in a reading is whether the message is truly meant to be shared. Just because spirit presents a piece of information does not mean it must be spoken aloud. Spirit communicates in layers. Some information is for the medium's awareness alone, to help them hold space more gently or steer the session with care.

Other messages are meant to be delivered, but with tact and sensitivity. And some are meant to be addressed only when the sitter is ready to receive them, not before. Discernment becomes the most vital tool in these moments. The medium must pause, breathe, and listen not only to spirit, but to their own inner guidance.

When abuse is revealed during a session, it often arrives indirectly. A medium may feel a deep sense of shame or fear that does not belong to them. They may see flashes of violent imagery, sense restriction in the throat or chest, or feel as though a child is hiding. Sometimes the spirit does not speak in words but in feeling.

The energy in the room shifts. The air grows heavy. The heart races. The medium may even feel sick. These are signs that the spirit is trying to express something that could not be said in life. The trauma that was held in silence is now rising through the energy field of the medium, asking for release.

Sometimes the spirit bringing the message is the perpetrator. Sometimes it is the victim. And sometimes it is neither, it is an ancestor or guide who is illuminating a pattern or truth that needs healing. The spirit of a grandmother may show that her daughter was abused, and that the trauma was never spoken of.

A child spirit may come through to express pain from violence they endured before death. In rare and complex cases, the very person who committed the abuse may step forward seeking forgiveness. These moments require extraordinary ethical clarity. They must never be rushed. They must never be used for dramatic effect. The safety and emotional well-being of the sitter must come first, always.

The medium must ask themselves not only what is being shown, but why. What is the purpose of this message? What is the healing that spirit is offering? What does the sitter need in order to process this? And most importantly, how can the medium speak with care without retraumatizing or overwhelming the person in front of them?

Words are powerful. When speaking of abuse, they must be chosen with precision and grace. It is never appropriate to say, "I see that your father molested you," even if the medium receives that information clearly. Instead, the medium might say, "There is something here that feels very painful, very private. I am sensing a boundary was violated in your past. Only if you feel ready, we can explore this together, gently." This leaves space for the sitter to remain in control of their experience.

Consent is essential. The sitter has the right to decline to explore what is being presented. The medium must respect that choice.

Mediumship is not an interrogation. It is an offering. The healing that comes from exposing abuse must always be guided by the person's readiness and autonomy. If the sitter says they do not want to talk about it, the medium should back away. Spirit will not force what the soul is not ready to process. Often, the mere acknowledgment that "something happened" is enough to begin the healing. The details are not always necessary.

For those who do choose to receive the full message, the impact can be profound. There is a deep validation that occurs when someone's unspoken pain is named. Many survivors of abuse have never been believed. Some were children who tried to speak but were silenced. Others were adults who carried their truth in secret, afraid of the consequences of telling.

When a medium gently brings that truth forward, it can be the first time the survivor feels seen. It can be the first time someone says, "I believe you," without question, without judgment, without expectation. This is not about fixing. It is about witnessing. And being witnessed in our pain is one of the most powerful forms of healing there is.

Spirit often brings messages of abuse not just for the individual, but for the entire lineage. Abuse rarely happens in isolation. It is often part of a generational pattern—unhealed trauma passed down through silence, control, addiction, secrecy, or violence.

One person speaking the truth can begin to dismantle that pattern. When a medium delivers a message that names the abuse, it is not just the sitter who is affected. The whole family system begins to shift. The energy that was bound in shame and fear begins to move. The possibility of healing enters the space where denial once reigned.

It is important to note that not every message about abuse is about revealing something the sitter already knows. Sometimes, spirit brings up abuse that the sitter has repressed or forgotten.

This can be dangerous if not handled with care. The medium must never try to force memory or suggest things that may lead the client to question their own experience in harmful ways. It is better to speak in symbols and feelings and allow the sitter to explore what arises for them in their own time. Mediumship is not therapy, and mediums must not act as therapists unless they are trained to do so. However, they can work in harmony with therapy, offering insight that supports and complements the healing process.

There is also the question of justice. Sometimes spirit brings forward messages not for emotional healing alone, but because they want to make wrongs right. This is especially true when the abuse was never acknowledged publicly or legally.

A victim may want their story known. A perpetrator may want to take responsibility. This can lead to complex ethical situations, especially if the accused is still alive. The medium must be cautious. They cannot accuse someone of abuse based solely on a message from spirit. They can, however, empower the sitter to trust their own knowing, to seek therapy, and to take whatever steps feel appropriate for their safety and healing.

When a perpetrator comes through asking for forgiveness, the medium must be exceptionally careful. Forgiveness is not owed. It cannot be demanded. The sitter may not be ready. They may never be ready. That is their right. The medium should never pressure the client to forgive, especially in the case of severe abuse.

Instead, they can say something like, "This spirit is expressing remorse for harm they caused. It is entirely your choice whether to receive that or not. You are not required to forgive. You are not responsible for their peace." This empowers the client to decide what feels right for them.

Mediums who carry their own histories of abuse may be particularly sensitive to these kinds of messages. They may be triggered. They may struggle to remain grounded. It is crucial for mediums to do their own healing work, to have supervision or support, and to know their limits.

Mediumship is not just about delivering messages. It is about being able to hold space for the emotional weight those messages carry. If the medium is overwhelmed or reactive, they cannot be fully present for the sitter.

Despite the difficulty, messages that bring abuse to light are some of the most important messages a medium can deliver. They break cycles of silence. They validate survivors. They allow the dead to take responsibility. They offer the living a chance to reclaim their power and they bring healing to wounds that have festered for generations. But this work must be done with integrity, compassion, and humility.

The medium must always remember that they are handling someone's most tender truth. They must speak as if holding a broken wing, gently, reverently, with the understanding that even a whisper can change a life.

Ultimately, when spirit brings abuse to light, it is not to destroy. It is to liberate. It is to bring the shadow into the light so that healing can begin. It is to say, "What happened matters." It is to say, "You are not alone." It is to say, "The truth will set you free."

Reflection Questions: When Spirit Brings Abuse to Light

1. How do I emotionally respond when a spirit or sitter brings up abuse; do I feel grounded, reactive, avoidant, or overwhelmed?

2. What personal wounds or memories might be activated in me when I witness or deliver messages involving trauma or violation?

3. Do I trust myself to hold space for this kind of pain and if not, what kind of support or training might I need?

4. Have I ever unintentionally bypassed or minimized a sitter's pain in an attempt to keep the message "light" or comfortable?

5. When a spirit acknowledges harm they caused in life, how do I discern whether their message is rooted in truth, remorse, or manipulation?

6. How do I ethically deliver information when the person receiving the message is unaware of or resistant to what's being revealed?

7. Do I feel pressure to "fix" emotional pain in a reading, or can I sit with the discomfort of what cannot be solved in that moment?

8. What spiritual beliefs do I hold about karma, healing, or justice and how might those beliefs influence how I interpret abusive energy?

9. When is it appropriate to continue the connection and when is it time to gently close the session for the safety of all involved?

10. Do I create time and space after difficult sessions to ground, debrief, or process what I have held?

11. Have I built a support system (peers, mentors, therapists) where I can reflect on the emotional weight of this work safely and without shame?

12. How do I honour the sacredness of truth-telling through mediumship, especially when that truth is hard, heavy, or hidden?

13. How can I ensure that my work as a medium never retraumatizes the sitter, but instead becomes a space where truth is honoured, and healing begins with compassion and care?

16. The Role of Forgiveness in Spirit Work

Forgiveness is one of the most misunderstood and yet most essential aspects of spiritual healing. In the context of mediumship, forgiveness often becomes the invisible thread that ties the living and the dead, the past and the present, the wound and the wisdom. It is not uncommon for a medium to find themselves standing in the heart of this tension, with a message from spirit that gently or sometimes urgently points to the need for resolution.

The soul that has passed may be carrying the weight of their own remorse. The soul that remains on Earth may be carrying the pain of betrayal, abandonment, or injustice. And in between them stands the medium, the witness to this sacred and complicated invitation to forgive.

Forgiveness in spirit work does not follow the rules of religion or societal conditioning. It is not about pretending nothing happened or absolving someone of responsibility. It is not about being the bigger person or suppressing rage. It is about liberation. At its core, forgiveness in mediumship is an energetic release. It is the unbinding of pain from the soul so that the spirit, whether living or dead, can continue their journey in freedom.

This release is not always mutual. Sometimes it comes from the spirit, asking for forgiveness. Sometimes it comes from the client, releasing the spirit from the grip of their resentment. And sometimes it does not come at all, because the time is not right, and that too is sacred.

When a spirit steps forward with remorse, it is usually felt immediately. The energy softens. The words spoken are not defensive or dramatic. There is no justification. There is only sincerity. The medium may feel this as a heaviness in the chest, or a wave of sorrow that rises without warning.

The spirit may admit their wrongs clearly, or they may struggle, caught in shame even beyond death. Some do not speak at all but show images that speak volumes, a slammed door, a hand raised, a child crying, a missed funeral. The medium becomes the translator of not just facts, but emotion. And in this delicate moment, they are tasked with offering the client a choice: to listen, to feel, and perhaps, to release.

But forgiveness cannot be forced. The medium must never suggest that a client must forgive in order to heal. That is not truth. Healing is personal. It unfolds in layers. Sometimes, forgiveness is not ready to bloom because the wound is still bleeding.

To ask someone to forgive prematurely is to dishonour their pain. The spirit may be ready to ask, but the client may not be ready to answer. That is not a failure. It is a process. Spirit understands this far more deeply than we do. Most spirits are not demanding absolution. They are simply seeking to speak their truth, to say, "I see now what I could not see then." That acknowledgment alone can be enough to begin the long and sacred road toward healing.

There are also times when the person in spirit never asked for forgiveness in life and perhaps would not ask for it even now. They may be stuck in their pride, or not yet fully awakened to the harm they caused. In such cases, the medium may be shown the truth of what happened, even without an apology.

The spirit may appear disoriented or confused or may not speak at all. The client may ask, "Why didn't they say they were sorry?" And in that absence, the weight of the wound may be felt even more sharply. This too must be met with honesty. The medium must not invent an apology for the sake of comfort. Instead, they must hold space for the truth and that sometimes closure does not come from the other side, but from within.

Forgiveness, then, becomes not a transaction but a choice. A sacred act of reclaiming one's power. The client may not have received justice in the physical world. They may never hear the words they longed for. But in choosing to release the cord that binds them to the one who harmed them, they are not saying what happened was acceptable. They are saying they are no longer willing to carry the burden.

Forgiveness is not a surrender to the abuser. It is a surrender to healing. It is saying, "I release this from my body, from my spirit, from my life." It is an act of profound courage.

Mediumship often reveals the interconnected nature of forgiveness across generations. An ancestor may step forward who never forgave their own parent. A spirit may speak of a pattern of harm that repeated through the lineage because no one stopped to heal it.

The client may discover that the rage they feel is not entirely theirs but inherited. The tears they cry may belong to their grandmother, their great-grandfather, to someone who never had the voice or the strength to release their pain. In these moments, forgiveness becomes an ancestral offering. It becomes an act of breaking the chain.

Ceremony can be a powerful support in this process. The medium may guide the client to write a letter to the spirit, expressing all that was never said. The letter may be burned in ritual, buried in the earth, or read aloud in a private moment of release. This gives voice to what was once unspeakable. It allows the energy to move.

The spirit may witness the ritual. They may respond. Or they may simply receive the message in silence, with reverence. There is no correct way to forgive. There is only the way that honours the truth of the soul.

There are times when forgiveness flows easily. The message from spirit is clear. The client feels a softening. Tears fall, and something opens. In those moments, healing is almost visible. You can feel it in the room. The temperature shifts. The air feels lighter.

Something has been unbound. And yet, this should not become the goal of every session. Forgiveness is not a performance. It cannot be manufactured. It must come from the heart.

It is also essential to understand that not all spirits ask for forgiveness in words. Some show their remorse through action.

They may act as protectors for the family they once hurt. They may guide the client toward healing. They may bring through specific details of what they now understand, offering validation without self-pity. Their presence is an apology. Their energy says, "I am here now in a different way." These moments can be deeply healing. The client may feel as though the person they once knew has finally become the person they needed.

But not all spirits transform immediately. Some remain unchanged. The client may feel disappointed, even angry, that the person who caused them harm seems oblivious or resistant.

The medium must honour that response. It is not their job to redeem the dead. It is their role to deliver the truth with compassion, and to hold space for whatever response arises. The client may choose to forgive on their own terms, or they may choose never to forgive at all. Both are valid. Both are sacred.

Forgiveness also has a shadow. There are times when people feel pressured to forgive in order to be spiritual. They are told that holding on to anger is low vibration, or that they will not heal unless they let go.

This is harmful and untrue. Anger is a valid emotion. It is a signal. It tells us that something was violated. To deny it is to deny the truth. The medium must never suggest that forgiveness is a requirement. It is an option, one that the soul will choose when and if it is ready.

When a client asks the medium, "Should I forgive them?" the most honest answer is, "That is entirely up to you." The medium may share what spirit has expressed. They may validate the client's pain. They may hold space for both the hurt and the healing. But they cannot answer that question on the client's behalf.

Forgiveness is deeply personal. It cannot be dictated.

Sometimes, the person in spirit is the one who was never forgiven in life. They may have died without reconciliation. They may have been estranged. They may carry regret. The medium may sense their longing to be heard. The client may feel torn. "I wanted to forgive them, but they died before I could." In these moments, spirit work becomes an opportunity for completion.

The medium can offer the space for that final exchange. A conversation across the veil. A resolution that transcends time.

There are also stories where the living seeks forgiveness from the dead. A client may come burdened with guilt. Perhaps they were not present when their loved one passed. Perhaps they spoke words they now regret. Perhaps they feel responsible for choices that led to pain. Spirit often responds with immense compassion in these cases.

They rarely hold blame. Most spirits have a wider view. They understand the complexity of life. They come not to punish, but to soothe. Their forgiveness is unconditional.

The medium becomes the conduit for this grace, allowing the client to release what they have carried.

In this way, forgiveness becomes a mirror. It reflects both ways. It heals both sides. It is not linear. It is not always mutual. But when it happens, it changes everything. It frees the energy. It lightens the soul. It restores what was fractured.

The medium must remember that they are not the agent of forgiveness. They are the witness. The vessel. The translator. Their task is not to decide who is right or wrong, but to hold space for the complexity of the human spirit. To offer the possibility of healing without forcing an outcome.

Forgiveness in spirit work is not about forgetting. It is about remembering differently. It is about seeing the whole story, not to excuse, but to understand. It is about reclaiming power, not surrendering it. It is about opening the door to peace, not erasing the pain that came before it.

There is a sacred beauty in this work. To watch a client weep as they finally feel seen. To hear them say, "I never thought I could let this go." To feel the shift when a spirit is released from shame. These are the quiet miracles of mediumship. They do not make headlines. They are not dramatic.

But they are real. They are the invisible transformations that ripple through families, through generations, through time.

In the end, forgiveness is not a destination. It is a path. A winding, personal, often messy path. And when spirit guides us along it, with truth and tenderness, it becomes one of the most powerful journeys we can take.

Staying true to your light means honouring the truth of who you are, even when the world around you tries to dim it. Your inner light is not something you earn or create—it is something you remember. It is the essence of your soul, your connection to divine love, and your compass through both joy and adversity.

To stay true to your light, you must learn to trust your intuition, your knowing, and the quiet voice within that reminds you of your worth and your purpose.

This is not always easy, especially in a world that rewards conformity and distractions. But your light was not meant to be hidden; it was meant to guide.

Remember, staying true to your light is not about being perfect or always feeling positive. It is about choosing to return to your centre, again and again, no matter how many times life pulls you away. It means making space for both light and shadow, holding compassion for your wounds, and allowing healing to be part of your brilliance.

Your light is sacred. It is the part of you that is connected to everything and everyone, yet it is also uniquely yours. Trust it. Feed it. Let it rise and lead.

Reflection Questions: The Role of Forgiveness in Spirit Work

1. What does forgiveness mean to me and how has that definition evolved through my spiritual work?

2. Have I ever received a message from spirit that asked me, or the sitter to forgive someone? How did that feel?

3. Do I believe that spirits can genuinely express remorse or seek redemption after death? Why or why not?

4. In what ways has mediumship softened my heart toward people I once felt resentment or pain toward?

5. Are there messages I have resisted delivering because I feared what forgiveness might awaken in the sitter or in myself?

6. When spirit brings forward an apology, do I believe it is always mine to accept or deliver?

7. Have I ever used forgiveness as a form of bypassing pain or conflict, rather than allowing myself to fully feel and heal?

8. What ancestral wounds in my family line may still be asking for forgiveness, across generations, cultures, or unspoken history?

9. How do I differentiate between authentic forgiveness and spiritual guilt or pressure to "let go"?

10. What emotions arise in me when I witness someone being asked to forgive a spirit who caused them pain?

11. Can forgiveness coexist with boundaries, justice, and truth, or do I see them as opposing forces?

12. Have I ever withheld forgiveness from myself, and how has that shaped my work as a medium?

13. In what ways has spirit offered me comfort or healing around moments in my past where I could not forgive, or be forgiven?

14. Do I carry any unresolved stories or energetic cords that might shift if forgiveness was offered, either from me or toward me?

15. Have I witnessed mediumship become a bridge for closure, peace, or reconciliation that was not possible in life?

16. When I sit with the energy of forgiveness, what does it feel like in my body; lightness, tension, grief, release?

17. How do my personal wounds shape the way I view forgiveness and am I ready to look at those with honesty?

18. What might it mean to forgive someone not because they "deserve" it, but because I deserve peace?

19. Can I accept that some sitters may never be ready to forgive and still hold space without judgment?

20. If spirit came today asking me to forgive someone I never expected, what part of me would resist, and what part would be relieved?

21. Do I believe that forgiveness can be an ongoing process, rather than a one-time act and how does this apply to spirit work?

22. What does it feel like when a spirit asks for forgiveness, but the sitter is not ready to receive or respond, how do I navigate that space?

23. Have I ever needed to forgive a spirit who was once close to me and what did that process look like within my own heart?

24. In what ways has forgiveness shown up in my dreams, visions, or ancestral communication?

25. Have I ever witnessed forgiveness bringing physical or emotional healing during or after a reading?

26. What role does self-forgiveness play in keeping my channel clear, open, and compassionate?

27. How do I hold space when a spirit expresses sorrow for something that can never be undone, how do I honour both truth and tenderness?

28. Are there moments where I've mistaken "letting go" for truly forgiving and what is the difference?

29. Can forgiveness extend beyond people to parts of myself, to old identities, or to times I abandoned my own truth?

30. What legacy do I want my own spirit to leave behind when I pass and how does forgiveness influence the energy I will one day carry forward?

17. Reparenting Through Spirit

There is a quiet ache that lives within many who walk the spiritual path. It is not always spoken aloud. It may not even be fully understood by the one who carries it. It is the ache of a childhood unmet. A longing for the love that was never given, the safety that was never offered, the validation that was never voiced.

This is not always about extreme trauma or overt neglect. Sometimes, it is about the small but repeated absences. The emotional unavailability. The parent who was physically present but emotionally distant. The caregiver who provided for needs but withheld affection. The environment where being sensitive, intuitive, or different was not understood, and often dismissed.

It is in these empty spaces that the soul begins to form the stories that follow us into adulthood: I am too much. I am not enough. I must earn love. I must hide who I really am.

Reparenting is the process of unlearning these beliefs and giving ourselves what was missing. It is not about blaming the past. It is about healing from it and in the sacred work of mediumship, reparenting often emerges not as a psychological technique, but as a deeply spiritual invitation.

Spirit steps forward not just with messages of comfort, but with acts of soul remembrance. The spirit world often becomes the parent we never had, or the mirror that shows us how to become that parent for ourselves. In this way, reparenting through spirit becomes a profound form of self-rescue.

For many clients, mediumship is the first time they feel truly seen. They sit before the medium, hoping for connection with a loved one, and instead are met with a love that transcends bloodlines and biology. They are told that their spirit guides have never left them, that their ancestors stand behind them with fierce protection, that their inner child is being cradled in light.

These are not just poetic images. They are real, energetic experiences. The soul receives what the psyche has longed for. And in that moment, something begins to rewire. The inner child who felt abandoned begins to feel held. The part of the adult that always had to be strong begins to soften. The medium becomes the channel through which this loving energy flows. Not as the source, but as the bridge.

The process of reparenting through spirit is not always soft and comforting. Sometimes, spirit brings forward tough love. A guide may step in and show the client the ways they are repeating old patterns. A grandmother in spirit may remind them that they are worthy of more than survival. A male ancestor may speak the words a father never said: I am proud of you.

These moments are often met with tears, not because the words are new, but because they are finally being heard. Mediumship allows for healing to occur on timelines that are not linear. What could not be said in the past can now be spoken in the sacred now.

One of the most powerful aspects of reparenting through spirit is the way it affirms the client's sensitivity. Many sensitive and intuitive people were raised in environments that did not understand or honour their gifts. As children, they were told to stop crying, to toughen up, to stop imagining things. Their empathy was treated as a weakness. Their connection to spirit, if expressed, may have been dismissed or even punished. Over time, they learned to suppress their gifts.

They learned that to be loved, they had to shrink. When a medium speaks directly to those gifts, when they say, "Spirit says you were always the seer, always the feeler," something deep inside awakens. The inner child lifts their head. The adult begins to reclaim the parts of themselves they buried. This is reparenting. This is resurrection.

Reparenting through spirit is not a replacement for therapy or clinical work. It is a complement. It works on the energetic and soul level, while therapeutic work may address the psychological and behavioural layers. Together, they form a holistic path to healing. The medium must know the difference. They are not there to diagnose or to analyse. They are there to offer sacred witnessing, to channel love, to be a mirror for the soul's potential. They offer what the child within never received: attention, validation, safety, belief.

It is important to understand that spirit does not always come through as the perfect parental figure. Sometimes, the very parent who wounded the client in life steps forward.

These moments are some of the most complex in mediumship. The client may feel torn between longing and pain, between the desire for connection and the anger of what was never acknowledged. If the parent in spirit expresses remorse, the client may feel relief, or they may feel rage. Both responses are valid. The medium must not try to rush forgiveness or harmony.

Instead, they must hold space for the truth. They may say, "Your father is showing me that he now sees the pain he caused. He says he was emotionally distant because he did not know how to love in the way you needed. He is asking to be heard, not to be excused." This opens the door for the client to respond in their own time, in their own way.

There are also times when the parent in spirit does not come through. This absence can be painful. The client may interpret it as another form of abandonment. But often, spirit withholds presence not as a punishment, but as a form of respect. The soul may not be ready. The medium may not be the right one for that message.

Or the healing may need to come through another channel, perhaps through a guide, or through the client's own inner work. Reparenting through spirit is not always about contact. Sometimes, it is about allowing space for the relationship to evolve in silence.

Spirit guides often play a vital role in reparenting. They step in as the archetypal mother, the wise father, the nurturer, the protector, the mentor.

They speak with patience, with gentleness, with strength. They teach the client how to listen to their own intuition, how to honour their needs, how to make choices that align with their truth. A guide may say, "It is safe now to rest. You do not have to fight anymore." Or "You are not too much. You were always meant to feel this deeply." These are the messages that rebuild a fractured foundation. These are the words that create a new internal compass.

Reparenting also involves learning to set boundaries. Many people who were not nurtured properly in childhood struggle to say no. They become caretakers, people pleasers, self-sacrificing to the point of collapse. Spirit often brings messages to interrupt this cycle. An ancestor may say, "You are allowed to protect your peace."

A guide may urge the client to stop rescuing others at their own expense. These are not just practical suggestions. They are acts of reparenting. They are the boundaries the child never learned to set, now being offered as a gift to the adult.

The body plays a central role in this process. The body is the archive of every unmet need. It holds the memories, the fears, the contractions. Reparenting through spirit includes helping the client reconnect with their body.

The medium may describe the way a spirit places their hand over the client's heart or wraps them in warmth. These images are not just symbolic. They are felt somatically. The nervous system responds. The body begins to release. This is not imagination. This is energetic reality.

Ritual is another important tool. Lighting a candle and calling on a guide to speak to the inner child. Writing letters to one's younger self, with the support of spirit. Creating a daily practice of sitting in silence and asking, "What do I need today that I did not receive then?" These small acts become sacred reparenting.

Mediums who carry their own inner child wounds may find this work especially powerful and at times, triggering. They must be aware of their own healing needs. They must do their own reparenting work so that they can hold others without projection. But they also have a unique gift. They understand the terrain. They know what it means to sit in longing. To ache for love. To rebuild from emptiness. Their empathy becomes a medicine. Their experience becomes a guidepost.

Reparenting through spirit is not about erasing the past. It is about reclaiming the self. It is about building a new foundation inside the body, inside the psyche, inside the soul. It is about giving the child within what was needed all along: safety, tenderness, presence, belief. It is about becoming the parent we deserved.

And spirit, in its infinite grace, often becomes our ally in this work. Not to do it for us, but to walk beside us. To whisper reminders. To bring the light when the night feels long. To say, "You are loved. You have always been loved." That is the truth at the core of reparenting through spirit. We are not alone. We were never meant to do this without support. And through mediumship, that support becomes real. Tangible. Healing.

Reflection Questions: Reparenting Through Spirit

1. In what ways have I felt emotionally or spiritually "unparented" in this life, and how has that shaped my sensitivity and needs?

2. Has spirit ever stepped in to give me the guidance, love, or safety I never received from a parent or caregiver?

3. When I connect with a nurturing guide, ancestor, or loved one in spirit, what part of me begins to feel held or reparented?

4. Do I allow myself to receive from spirit, not just messages, but comfort, protection, and support?

5. What beliefs about love, safety, and worth were shaped by my upbringing and how do those beliefs affect my spiritual path?

6. How do I speak to my inner child now? Is it with judgment, indifference, or tenderness?

7. What rituals or mediumship practices help me feel "parented" by something greater than myself?

8. Have I ever projected unmet parental needs onto spirit, or expected them to heal what I am still afraid to face?

9. What part of me is still waiting to be chosen, seen, or protected and how can I offer that presence to myself now?

10. When I sit with someone else's grief or trauma, how do I tend to my own inner child before and after?

11. In what ways do I confuse performance, over giving, or perfectionism with being worthy of love?

12. Can I hold space for spirit to reparent me without needing it to look like the love I lost or longed for?

13. What boundaries, routines, or soothing practices can I give myself that my child self never had?

14. How does spirit model the type of parenting I needed gentle, wise, unconditional, present?

15. What would it look like to become the parent my inner child has been waiting for, with spirit walking beside me?

18. Soul Retrieval and Fragmentation

There are moments in life so painful, so overwhelming, that a part of the soul retreats. It steps out of the body, out of the timeline, and into a space where it can remain untouched by the horror that occurred. This is not weakness. It is wisdom.

The soul knows when something is too much to bear. It knows when to shield itself. This retreat is what many spiritual traditions refer to as soul fragmentation. It is not a flaw or a failure. It is a survival response. And for the medium who works deeply with spirit and energy, it is an essential truth to understand.

Soul fragmentation occurs in moments of intense trauma. Abuse, neglect, violence, betrayal, sudden loss, these experiences can rupture the continuity of the soul's presence within the body. The part that splits off does so to protect innocence, to preserve identity, to prevent the total collapse of the being.

These fragments are not lost. They are simply displaced. They exist in energetic suspension, waiting for a time when it is safe to return. But until they do, the person may walk through life feeling hollow, confused, disconnected, or stuck in patterns they cannot seem to break.

Mediumship, when practiced with depth and care, becomes a powerful tool for soul retrieval. It is not that the medium goes out searching for soul pieces in distant realms. Rather, it is that spirit often brings attention to the parts of a person that have been left behind.

Spirit may guide the client to remember moments they buried. Spirit may show the child who went silent after the assault, or the teenager who disappeared inward after the grief of a parent's death.

These are not simply memories. These are soul states, whole aspects of self that have not reintegrated into the present moment.

The medium becomes the witness to this soul landscape, and through that witnessing, a doorway to return is opened.

Soul retrieval is not about forcing these parts to come back. It is about invitation. The lost parts of self are often guarded by fear, shame, or grief. They must be approached gently. Spirit often does this with images of safety. A guide may show the client as a child being held in light.

An ancestor may wrap the fragment in a blanket and rock it back to the heart. These visions are not fantasies. They are energetic messages. They are the way spirit communicates the healing that is available. The client may cry, may tremble, may feel a deep sense of homecoming. These are signs that something real is occurring.

Fragmentation also shows up in the body. A person with soul loss may experience chronic dissociation, numbness, fatigue, or memory lapses. They may say things like, "I do not feel like myself," or "It is like I am watching my life from the outside." These are not just emotional states. They are energetic conditions. The soul is not fully anchored. Mediumship sessions often begin to restore that anchoring.

When the medium validates the pain, when they acknowledge what was never spoken, the body begins to feel safe again. Safety is the first requirement for soul pieces to return. Spirit knows this. That is why their messages often focus on love, on belonging, on remembrance. They are creating the container for return.

There are also spiritual contracts involved in soul fragmentation. Sometimes, the part that split off holds a specific energy, a gift, a sensitivity, a power. That part may have left because it was not safe to express that gift in the environment the person was in. The child who could see spirits may have shut that ability down because it frightened the adults around them. The young woman who felt deep empathy may have learned to numb because her emotions were mocked.

These soul fragments are not just aspects of identity. They are carriers of medicine. When they return, they often bring a gift. But that gift cannot be received until the wound is addressed.

The medium's role in soul retrieval is not to perform the retrieval themselves. Rather, it is to serve as a guide, a witness, a voice for the process that is already happening in the soul. The medium may be shown the moment the fragment left. They may describe the age, the environment, the emotion.

They may say, "Spirit is showing me a seven-year-old you, sitting under a table, feeling invisible." The client often responds with recognition. The tears rise. The memory stirs. And in that moment, the adult self reaches for the child self. The bridge is built. The reintegration begins.

This process must be supported with grounding. The client may feel raw, exposed, even overwhelmed after a session that touches on soul fragmentation. The medium should always offer closing rituals, grounding practices, and aftercare guidance. It is not enough to open the wound. The space must be held afterward. Spirit often participates in this too. Guides may place energy around the client.

Ancestors may bless the heart. The work is both tender and sacred. It is not something to rush.

Soul fragmentation can also occur across lifetimes. The soul does not forget what it has experienced, even if the conscious mind does. A client may carry wounds from a past life where they were persecuted, enslaved, or betrayed. These wounds can influence current behaviour.

Fear of visibility, distrust of intimacy, chronic guilt, these may all stem from soul parts that split off in other timelines. Spirit often reveals these fragments not as past life stories for curiosity's sake, but as keys to healing. When the client understands the origin of the pattern, they can begin to unhook from it.

The medium may describe a past life where the client lost a child and never recovered. The grief of that life may be repeating in this one. By acknowledging it, by bringing love to it, the soul begins to release. The fragment returns.

Rituals of soul retrieval are powerful ways to support this process. The client may be guided to create a sacred space, light a candle, call on their guides, and speak to the part of themselves that is missing. They may say, "You are safe now. You are wanted. You are allowed to come home." These words carry power. They are heard not just by the conscious mind, but by the soul.

Spirit often responds by amplifying the energy. The client may feel warmth, pressure in the heart, or a sudden sense of wholeness. This is not imagination. This is restoration.

Not all soul fragments are ready to return immediately. Some remain at a distance until the body and psyche are prepared to hold them. The medium must honour this. They must not push or promise. Instead, they offer the message and trust that the process will unfold in divine timing.

Sometimes, the session is the first step in a longer journey. The client may begin to dream of the lost parts. They may be drawn to certain music, places, or rituals. These are the soul's way of preparing for return.

Fragmentation is also common in those who have experienced spiritual trauma. People who were raised in environments where their spiritual nature was shamed, suppressed, or manipulated may have rejected core parts of their soul. They may feel cut off from their own intuition, from the divine, from trust.

Spirit often brings healing by reminding them of who they were before the conditioning. A guide may say, "You were always connected. They just made you forget." These messages reignite the inner light. They call the soul back to its original state.

Mediums who carry their own history of soul fragmentation must be especially aware of their energy. This work can stir old wounds. But it can also be deeply affirming. The more a medium reclaims their own fragments, the more they can help others do the same. Their sensitivity becomes their compass.

Their journey becomes their medicine.

Soul retrieval is not a one-time event. It is a lifelong path. The soul reveals itself in layers. Each return brings more clarity, more wholeness, more vitality. The person begins to feel more themselves than they ever have. They begin to make choices from alignment rather than trauma. They begin to speak with their true voice.

Spirit celebrates these moments. They are not dramatic. They are quiet revolutions.

Ultimately, soul retrieval is the sacred act of coming home to the self. Mediumship, when practiced with love and integrity, becomes a key to that return. It opens the door to the places we forgot. It shines light on the parts we abandoned. It reminds us that nothing is truly lost.

The soul waits. The soul remembers and with love, with patience, with spirit as our guide, the soul returns.

19. Spirit-Led Integration and Embodiment

Healing through mediumship is not complete until the wisdom received becomes lived experience. Words, messages, insights, and even profound moments of soul contact mean very little if they are not brought into the body, into the breath, into the decisions a person makes. Mediumship is not just about receiving information from spirit. It is about integrating that information into daily life and embodying the healing that spirit offers. Spirit-led integration and embodiment are the final steps of the sacred cycle. They are where everything becomes real.

Many people come to mediums seeking clarity or comfort. They hope to hear from a loved one, to understand a relationship, to find answers about their path. Often, they leave the session with powerful messages and a renewed sense of connection. But what happens next is what truly matters. Spirit does not speak to entertain. Spirit speaks to evolve. And that evolution is not theoretical. It is felt in the bones, in the nervous system, in the choices made once the session is over.

Integration is the process of allowing the energy of the spirit message to unfold over time. It is not a mental activity, though the mind often tries to control it. Integration happens when a person makes space for what they have received to settle, to breathe, and to speak again in quieter ways.

Spirit messages often arrive in powerful waves during a reading, but their meaning deepens afterward. Days or weeks later, the client may suddenly feel a layer of emotion they were not ready to access before. A phrase from the reading may echo in their dreams. They may begin to see synchronicities that guide them toward a choice they had previously avoided. All of this is integration. All of this is spirit continuing to work.

The medium has a responsibility to support integration. They must remind the client that the session is a beginning, not a conclusion. They may suggest practices such as journaling, meditation, rest, and time in nature. They may encourage the client to revisit the recording or notes from the session over time. They may share that certain emotions or memories may surface in the days following the reading, and that this is part of the healing.

By normalizing the process of unfolding, the medium empowers the client to stay engaged with the spirit connection beyond the moment of contact.

Embodiment is where integration becomes lived truth. It is where the message of spirit begins to reshape the way the person moves in the world. A client who has been told by their grandmother in spirit that they are loved exactly as they may begin to speak more kindly to themselves.

They may stop chasing external validation. A person who has received a message of forgiveness from a deceased parent may begin to open their heart in new ways. They may allow themselves to be more vulnerable in their relationships.

These are not dramatic changes. They are subtle shifts in being. But over time, they create a new reality. This is the miracle of embodiment.

Spirit often offers guidance on how to embody the healing they bring. They may suggest rituals, daily practices, or changes in lifestyle. They may encourage the client to write, to move, to rest, to speak up, or to let go. These suggestions are not rules. They are invitations. The client must discern what resonates and what does not. The key is to remain open to the idea that spirit's messages are not static. They are dynamic, alive, evolving. And they require participation.

The body plays a central role in embodiment. For healing to be fully integrated, the body must be part of the conversation. This is especially important for clients who have experienced trauma. Trauma lives in the body, not just in the mind.

Spirit often addresses this by bringing messages that help the client reconnect with their physical self. A guide may say, "Breathe deeper. Your body is tired of bracing." Or, "Move your hips. Dance your sorrow. Let it out." These are not metaphors. They are instructions for liberation. The body holds what the soul is trying to express. When the body is allowed to participate, the healing deepens.

Many people live dissociated from their bodies due to pain, shame, or conditioning. Mediumship can serve as a re-entry point. When spirit validates the client's physical or emotional experience, the body relaxes. The person begins to trust themselves again. They may cry for the first time in years. They may feel hunger, pleasure, or fatigue they had been ignoring. These are signs that the spirit is not only speaking through the medium but through the body of the client. The body becomes the oracle.

Embodiment also means making choices aligned with the soul's truth. This may require the client to set boundaries, end toxic relationships, change careers, or finally pursue the calling they have been avoiding. Spirit will often nudge but not force. They will say,

"You know what you need to do," and leave space for the client to choose.

The medium must hold this space without trying to control the outcome. They are not there to give advice. They are there to translate the wisdom of spirit and to trust the client's own authority to act.

There are times when the process of embodiment is delayed. A client may receive a powerful message but feel afraid to act on it. They may not yet believe they are worthy of the healing offered.

This is where patience is essential. Spirit is not in a rush. The message will return again and again, in dreams, in synchronicities, in the quiet pull of the heart. The soul does not give up on itself. The medium must trust this process and remind the client that healing does not expire. It unfolds in divine timing.

Rituals can be powerful tools for integration and embodiment. Lighting a candle each morning and asking, "How can I live in alignment today?" Taking a walk and letting the feet repeat the message received: "You are loved. You are seen. You are enough."

Writing the message in a journal, drawing it, singing it, speaking it aloud—these acts give the energy a place to live. They move the healing from the intangible to the tangible. They root the message in the now.

Spirit also works with archetypes during integration. A message from a guide may carry the energy of the mother, the warrior, the teacher, the healer. The client may begin to feel those aspects awaken within them. They may begin to embody a more nurturing presence, a stronger voice, a clearer sense of truth.

These archetypes are not external figures. They are soul qualities being remembered. Mediumship becomes a mirror, reflecting the client back to themselves. Integration means reclaiming these forgotten parts.

It is important to acknowledge that integration and embodiment may bring discomfort. When a person begins to change, the people around them may resist. Old dynamics may be challenged. Relationships may shift. Spirit often prepares the client for this. A guide may say, "Not everyone will understand your path, but it is still yours to walk." The medium must affirm this truth.

Growth is not always met with applause. Sometimes it is met with silence or judgment. But the soul knows when it is on track. The body knows too. That deep sense of resonance, of rightness, is the compass. It is the sign that integration is real.

Mediums must also walk this path themselves. It is not enough to deliver messages to others. The medium must also ask, "What am I integrating? What am I embodying?" They must allow spirit to teach them, challenge them, and shape them.

Their own embodiment becomes their authority. Not perfection, but presence. The more they live the truth of the messages they deliver, the more powerful their work becomes. Embodiment is the foundation of integrity.

There are moments in mediumship when the message is so clear, so precise, that the client has no doubt it is real. But the deeper miracle is when that message becomes part of the client's life. When they stop apologizing for their existence.

When they begin to trust their own intuition. When they choose love over fear. This is the fruit of spirit work. Not just clarity, but transformation. Not just connection, but embodiment.

Spirit-led integration is gentle, patient, wise. It does not demand. It invites. It knows that the soul is always ready, even when the mind is afraid. It knows that healing happens in spirals, not in straight lines. It knows that every step toward embodiment is a step toward freedom. And it celebrates every choice made from truth.

In the end, the work of the medium is not just to speak for the dead. It is to awaken the living. It is to help people remember who they are and to give them the tools to live from that place. Integration and embodiment are where that remembering becomes reality. Where the soul comes home. Where spirit is not just heard but lived.

20. The Future of Mediumship

Mediumship has always been a bridge between the worlds. It has walked quietly through the temples of the ancients, spoken in riddles at the edges of sacred fires, hidden in the hearts of mystics, prophets, and wise ones. It has survived persecution, ridicule, and centuries of fear. It has been disguised as prophecy, wrapped in religious ecstasy, and whispered in the corners of grief-stricken homes.

Despite all that, it endures. Mediumship continues because it speaks to something eternal. It responds to a longing that cannot be denied the longing to know that life does not end, that love endures, that the soul remembers. As we stand now at a threshold between worlds, between old paradigms and emerging consciousness; the question is no longer whether mediumship will survive. It is how it will evolve.

The future of mediumship is rooted in authenticity. Gone are the days when theatrics and vague generalities could pass as evidence. The collective is awakening, and with it comes a demand for depth, truth, and integrity.

Mediums of the future are not here to perform. They are here to serve. They will be soul-informed, trauma-aware, and energetically precise. They will understand that what they are offering is not entertainment. It is medicine. Their words will carry the frequency of healing. Their presence will anchor remembrance. Their role will not be to prove anything, but to remind humanity of what it already knows, that we are not alone, that love is indestructible, that death is not the end.

One of the greatest shifts occurring in mediumship is the merging of spiritual practice with psychological awareness.

Mediums can no longer afford to separate the spiritual from the emotional or the psychic from the somatic. The most profound messages are often those that speak directly to a person's unhealed wounds, outdated narratives, and inherited beliefs.

Mediums who understand trauma, nervous system regulation, attachment theory, and shadow work will be better equipped to deliver messages in ways that actually support transformation. Spirit does not bypass the human. Spirit works through it. And the mediums of tomorrow will be required to meet both spirit and the human in front of them with equal reverence.

Training and mentorship will evolve. The future will demand more than weekend workshops and surface-level certifications. Mediumship education will become more rigorous, more holistic, and more rooted in ethical and embodied practice.

Students will learn not just how to open to spirit, but how to close, how to ground, how to hold space for grief, how to navigate projection, and how to regulate their own systems. There will be a return to lineage, to initiation, to the ancient understanding that this is not just a gift. It is a sacred responsibility.

Mentors will be required to do their own inner work, to model humility, and to recognize that every medium has a unique path to walk.

Technology will also play a role. Virtual sessions, digital spaces, and global communities will allow mediums to reach more people than ever before. But with that reach comes responsibility. The digital realm must not dilute the depth of the work.

Ethical standards will need to be upheld. Mediums will need to discern when technology supports connection and when it interferes. Authentic presence cannot be replaced by algorithms. The soul is not a data point. The future will require a balance, using technology to share the message while keeping the message rooted in heart, truth, and spirit.

Another profound shift will be the collective recognition that mediumship is not reserved for the chosen few. The age of the gatekeeper is dissolving. Mediumship is an innate capacity within all human beings. Some may have a natural sensitivity.

Others may awaken their gifts through loss, spiritual practice, or inner healing. But the message is the same, this is not about hierarchy. It is about remembrance. The future of mediumship will involve guiding people back to their own connection with the unseen. Mediums will become facilitators, teachers, and mentors who empower others to hear, feel, and trust the language of their own soul.

The relationship with spirit guides will deepen and become more nuanced. Mediums will no longer view guides as external authorities but as aspects of a larger spiritual intelligence working in cooperation with the medium's higher self. The work will become more collaborative, more integrated.

Mediums will learn to recognize the archetypal nature of certain guides, to honor ancestral influence, and to respect the multidimensional nature of the spirit realm. Guides will not be treated as accessories or characters in a performance. They will be honoured as sacred companions in the work of human evolution.

Death education will become a central part of mediumship's future.

As the collective begins to confront mortality more directly, there will be a greater need for spiritual midwives and mediums who can support the dying, comfort the grieving, and offer insight into the afterlife. End-of-life care will become more holistic.

Mediums may be called into hospices, hospitals, and private homes. Their role will not be to predict or to impress, but to hold space for crossing over, to listen for the whispers of spirit, and to help families connect with their loved ones in ways that are meaningful and real. Death will no longer be feared but honoured as a sacred passage.

Mediumship will also intersect with collective healing. The spirits of ancestors, of the land, of the forgotten and the silenced will come forward more and more.

Mediums will be asked to listen not only for individual messages, but for the voices of history, lineage, and culture. The work will expand to include the healing of generational trauma, the honouring of indigenous wisdom, and the remembrance of spiritual traditions that were once lost or suppressed.

Mediumship will no longer be seen as personal. It will be recognized as a tool for collective awakening, a way to restore balance where it was broken, to speak the names of the unheard, and to walk with justice as well as compassion.

The ethics of mediumship will become more defined. Consent, boundaries, and client empowerment will be emphasized. Mediums will need to become fluent not just in spiritual language, but in psychological safety. They will need to know how to respond to clients who are vulnerable, grieving, or navigating mental health challenges.

They will need to know when to refer, when to pause, and when silence is more sacred than speech. The days of shock value and vague validation are fading. The future calls for precision, compassion, and deep listening. The client will no longer be a passive receiver, but an active participant in the dialogue with spirit.

Mediums themselves will be expected to engage in continual personal growth. The days of claiming authority based on channelling alone are ending.

Mediums will be asked, "Are you walking your talk? Are you embodying what you speak?" Their credibility will not come from their followers, but from their integrity. Spirit will align with those who are committed to their own evolution.

The gift will not be withheld from those who stumble, but it will become clearer in the hands of those who are willing to be humbled, to learn, to apologize, and to keep walking.

The future of mediumship will also embrace diversity. The spirit world does not discriminate. Love comes in all forms, and messages from spirit are for everyone—regardless of race, gender identity, culture, or spiritual background. Mediumship must reflect this truth. It must expand beyond the western, often whitewashed lens through which it has long been filtered.

Voices from many traditions, from many lands, from many lineages will rise. Mediums will need to listen, to decolonize their practice, to honour where their teachings come from, and to uplift voices that have been marginalized. Spirit is inclusive. Mediumship must be too.

There will also be a deeper exploration of multidimensional mediumship. Messages will not only come from the deceased but from the higher self, from parallel timelines, from galactic energies, and from realms beyond the sixth dimension.

Mediums will become translators of frequency, not just personality. They will speak not only of who the spirit was in life, but of what the soul is becoming in eternity. The work will become more expansive, more layered. But always, it will return to the heart. The more cosmic the work becomes, the more grounded it must be in love.

Ultimately, the future of mediumship is not just about communication. It is about transformation. Spirit does not come to confirm what we already know. Spirit comes to awaken us to what we have forgotten.

The messages are not the destination. They are the beginning. Mediums are not just messengers. They are mirrors, catalysts, companions. Their work is to walk beside others as they remember who they are, as they reclaim their soul, as they live their truth.

And what of the medium themselves? In the future, the medium will be less of a persona and more of a presence. They will be the quiet ones who know how to listen. The grounded ones who carry both the light and the shadow with grace.

The wise ones who know that the veil is thin not just in death, but in every moment, we choose love over fear. They will be students of life, servants of the soul, and keepers of the sacred. They will not need titles or stages. Their authority will be felt in the way they hold space, in the way they speak truth, in the way they live in alignment.

Mediumship is not going anywhere. It is evolving. And the evolution is beautiful. It is raw, real, and radiant. It is no longer about proving life after death. It is about helping people truly live. The future of mediumship is not in the stars. It is in the breath. It is in the heart. It is in the simple act of presence and in that presence, everything becomes possible.

Reflection Questions: The Future of Mediumship

1. What kind of medium do I want to become; not just in skill, but in integrity, presence, and emotional depth?

2. How is the role of the medium changing in today's world, and what does that evolution ask of me?

3. Am I willing to let go of outdated ideas or performative models of mediumship to embrace a more grounded and human approach?

4. What does ethical, trauma-informed, heart-cantered mediumship look like and how do I embody that in my practice?

5. How can I contribute to the next generation of mediums through teaching, mentoring, or simply leading by example?

6. In what ways can technology, psychology, and spiritual wisdom work together to support the evolution of this sacred practice?

7. What wounds must be healed in the spiritual community for mediumship to become safer, more truthful, and more respected?

8. Am I willing to continue growing, unlearning, and expanding, even when it challenges my comfort or identity as a medium?

9. What does spirit seem to be calling me toward as a future direction in my own path and am I listening?

10. If I were to leave a legacy as a medium, what would I want it to be remembered for?

21. The Ego in Mediumship

The relationship between the ego and mediumship is one of the most complex and important aspects of spiritual development. It is also one of the most misunderstood. In spiritual circles, the ego is often treated as something to be eliminated, silenced, or overcome. It is portrayed as the enemy of the soul, the obstacle to truth, and the cause of all suffering.

But this oversimplification ignores the essential role the ego plays in the human experience, and more importantly, in the path of the medium. To be an embodied channel for spirit, one must first come to terms with the ego, not by destroying it, but by refining it, humbling it, and aligning it with service.

The ego is the part of the self that is responsible for identity, protection, and separation. It gives us a sense of who we are in relation to others. It defines our preferences, our goals, our fears, and our stories. It is necessary for survival. Without an ego, we would not be able to distinguish ourselves from others.

We would not be able to assert boundaries, set intentions, or navigate the complexities of human life. In this way, the ego is not an enemy. It is a developmental necessity.

For the medium, however, the ego can become a powerful filter. It can shape the way spirit is interpreted, received, and delivered. It can distort messages to serve its own need for validation or control. It can insert doubt or overconfidence. It can create a performance instead of a sacred offering.

The ego in mediumship is not inherently bad, but it is inherently influential. If not recognized and worked with consciously, it can lead the medium astray.

There are many faces of the ego within the mediumship space. One of the most common is the desire to be right. The medium may feel pressure to deliver exact names, dates, or details in order to prove their legitimacy. While evidence is a vital part of ethical mediumship, it becomes problematic when the medium's self-worth is tied to the performance.

A reading then becomes a test of the medium's ability, rather than an act of service to the sitter and the spirit. The ego says, "I must be right to be valuable." The soul says, "I offer what is here, without needing it to be perfect."

Another face of ego is the desire to be seen as special. Many mediums unconsciously build identities around their gifts. They may speak as though they are chosen or more evolved than others. This can create separation and hierarchy. The truth is that mediumship is a gift, yes, but it is also a role.

It does not make the medium better, wiser, or more important than anyone else. It simply means they are wired in a particular way to receive and translate energy. The ego seeks elevation. The soul seeks humility. When a medium begins to believe their gift makes them superior, the channel becomes clouded with self-importance.

The wounded ego can also manifest in the fear of being wrong. Some mediums avoid taking risks in their readings because they fear judgment or criticism. They may play it safe, speak in vague terms, or seek constant affirmation from their clients. This is not a sign of spiritual weakness. It is a sign of human vulnerability. The fear of failure is deeply rooted in the ego's need for safety and approval.

The medium who has not yet made peace with failure may find themselves drained, anxious, or stuck in self-doubt after every session. Healing this requires compassion, not condemnation.

There is also the martyr ego, the part of the medium that feels they must suffer to serve. This can look like over-giving, undercharging, or ignoring one's own boundaries. The ego says, "I must sacrifice myself to be worthy of this gift." But spirit never asks for self-destruction. Spirit asks for presence.

Mediums must learn to separate the ego's stories of worthiness from the actual sacred nature of their work. They must allow themselves to receive, to rest, to be human.

Working with the ego in mediumship requires awareness. The first step is to recognize when the ego is active. This is not always easy. The ego is subtle and deeply conditioned. It may show up as comparison with other mediums, as jealousy, as fear of criticism, or as the need to prove one's connection.

It may show up as a desire to dominate the reading, to control the outcome, or to seek validation from the sitter. These are not signs of failure. They are signs of humanity. The key is to observe without judgment.

Meditation, shadow work, and self-inquiry are essential tools for working with the ego. They help the medium become familiar with their own patterns, wounds, and needs. When a medium knows their own triggers, they are less likely to project them into their work. They can notice when they are speaking from a wound rather than from spirit. They can pause, breathe, and return to the energy of service. This is not about being perfect. It is about being present.

Another powerful practice is humility. Humility does not mean thinking less of oneself. It means thinking of oneself less often. It means placing the work, the message, and the connection above the desire for praise or control. Humility creates spaciousness in the channel. It invites spirit to speak more clearly. A humble medium says, "I do not need to be the centre. I am here to be a vessel." This surrender opens the field for deeper healing.

Feedback is also essential. Mediums must be willing to hear when they are off-track. They must be open to learning, to refining their delivery, to receiving guidance from mentors, clients, and spirit alike. The ego resists feedback. The soul welcomes it. A medium who invites feedback is a medium who continues to grow. They are not rigid. They are in flow.

The community also plays a role in shaping the ego. Mediums need spaces where they are supported, challenged, and kept accountable. Too often, the spiritual field fosters isolation. Mediums are placed on pedestals or treated as infallible. This creates distortion. Mediums need spiritual friendships, councils, and communities where they can speak honestly about their doubts, their growth edges, and their humanity. In these spaces, the ego softens. It is seen, held, and transformed.

The ego is not just personal. It is collective. Mediums also carry the cultural ego, the inherited beliefs about what it means to be spiritual, successful, or seen. In a society that rewards visibility, applause, and achievement, the medium must constantly return to their centre. They must ask, "Why am I doing this? Who is this really for?"

When the answer is truth, connection, and love, the ego rests. When the answer is status or validation, the ego tightens. This is a dance. It is not something to conquer, but to become intimate with.

It is also important to acknowledge the positive roles of ego in mediumship. The ego gives the medium the courage to speak. It creates the sense of identity needed to hold space, to create structure, and to navigate relationships with clients. A healthy ego allows the medium to say no, to take up space, and to share their message with confidence. It is not about getting rid of the ego. It is about aligning it with soul.

When the ego and the soul are in harmony, the work becomes luminous. The medium feels both grounded and guided. They are able to step forward without arrogance and step back without fear. They can say, "This is what I am hearing," without needing it to be received in any particular way. They can own their role while knowing they are not the source, only the instrument. This balance is sacred. It is the foundation of sustainable, ethical, and powerful mediumship.

Spirit also supports the refining of the ego. Guides will often challenge the medium when the ego begins to dominate. They may withdraw slightly, offer silence, or bring through messages that confront the medium's illusions. This is not punishment. It is love. Spirit wants the medium to grow. They will not collude with the ego's need for control. They will gently invite surrender. And in that surrender, deeper truth arises.

The evolution of the medium is not a straight line. There will be times when the ego flares, when old wounds rise, when the need to prove or protect takes over. These moments are invitations to return to the heart. They are not failures. They are initiations. The ego is not a flaw in the design. It is part of the path. When honoured and understood, it becomes a servant to the soul.

In the end, the goal is not to transcend the ego, but to integrate it. To walk with it, not behind it. To allow it to have a seat at the table, but not the head of it. The ego can hold the microphone, but the message must come from spirit. This is the work. This is the practice. And in that practice, the medium becomes not only a channel for the other side, but a bridge between heaven and earth, spirit and self, truth and love.

Reflection Questions: The Ego in Mediumship

1. Do I ever feel the need to prove my ability as a medium, and what fear or wound might that need be covering?

2. When someone validates my reading, do I feel relief, pride, or pressure to keep performing at that level?

3. How do I respond internally when a reading does not go as expected? Do I blame myself, the sitter, or spirit?

4. Am I able to fully surrender to spirit during a reading, or do I try to control, shape, or steer the message?

5. Have I ever felt jealousy or comparison toward other mediums, and what might that be reflecting back to me?

6. Do I sometimes confuse spiritual identity with self-worth? Who am I without my gift?

7. What part of me feels uncomfortable with not knowing, and how does ego respond when mystery cannot be explained?

8. Do I secretly fear being wrong, rejected, or irrelevant in my spiritual work? How do I meet that fear with compassion?

9. Have I ever used my role as a medium to feel important, needed, or spiritually superior?

10. In what ways has humility deepened my connection to spirit, and where am I still learning to let go?

11. How do I differentiate between my intuition and my ego voice, and which one do I trust more often?

12. Can I receive feedback or criticism without defensiveness or does my ego take it as a personal attack?

13. What does true service mean to me and how do I know when I have stepped out of service and into self-seeking?

14. When do I feel most aligned with my higher self during readings, and what conditions support that alignment?

15. What spiritual practices help me quiet the ego and return to the heart of my mediumship?

22. The Role of Dreams and the Subconscious in Mediumship

Mediumship exists not only in the waking world but also in the sacred landscape of dreams. The dream state is one of the most potent and unfiltered spaces where spirit can reach the soul directly. During sleep, the conscious mind relaxes, the rational defences soften, and the subconscious opens. In this receptive state, the soul becomes more available for communion with the unseen.

It is here, in the mystery of night, that many people receive their first spirit visits, messages, warnings, and visions. Dreams are the forgotten language of the soul, and for the medium, they are an essential part of the path.

In psychological terms, the dream state is a bridge to the subconscious. It reveals our unprocessed emotions, our shadow selves, our unmet desires, and the deep archetypal stories that shape our perception of reality. Dreams carry symbols from the collective unconscious, offering messages that were both personal and universal.

These symbols, when interpreted with care, could lead to profound healing and self-awareness. In spiritual terms, dreams serve a similar purpose. They hold space for healing that cannot yet occur in the conscious mind. They bring unresolved emotions to the surface and act as vessels for soul communication.

Mediums who learn to work with their dreams expand their capacity to receive spirit not just through clair senses in waking life, but through the dream field as well.

Many mediumistic initiations begin with dreams. A person might begin dreaming of deceased loved ones, guides, or places they have never seen in this lifetime. These dreams often carry a different texture. They feel more real than dreams. The colours are more vivid, the messages are clearer, and the emotional impact lingers for days. This is not imagination. This is spirit using the dream state as a doorway. When the conscious mind is too resistant or afraid to receive a message, the spirit will often choose the back door of the subconscious.

The soul recognizes truth even when the personality is not ready.

Spirit visitation dreams are distinct from regular dreams. They tend to have a calm, steady energy. The deceased appear as healthy, radiant versions of themselves. There is often direct eye contact and a clear message or emotional exchange.

Sometimes the spirit speaks. Sometimes they simply appear, radiating love and peace. The dream may end with a sense of closure or release. These dreams are not always dramatic. Often, they are simple and deeply comforting. Spirit visitation dreams are more than just dreams. They are real encounters that occur on a soul level.

The subconscious mind plays a powerful role in mediumship because it is the storehouse of all unprocessed material. This includes grief, trauma, ancestral patterns, unexpressed emotion, and intuitive knowing. The conscious mind filters and edits. The subconscious receives and records.

When a medium learns to access their subconscious, they gain access to a deeper layer of spiritual truth. They begin to recognize patterns not only in their own psyche, but in the messages they receive for others.

The medium who understands their own subconscious landscape is far less likely to project their wounds into their readings. They become clear, compassionate, and self-aware channels.

Dreamwork is one of the most powerful practices a medium can adopt. It begins with intention. Before sleep, the medium might say, "I am open to receiving guidance from spirit tonight. I invite only love, truth, and clarity into my dreams." Keeping a dream journal beside the bed allows the medium to capture impressions immediately upon waking.

The details may fade quickly, but the emotional energy and symbolic content often carry vital information. Over time, patterns emerge. Certain symbols repeat. Guides may introduce themselves. Specific themes may surface again and again. The dream journal becomes a map of the soul's journey.

Symbols in dreams are highly personal but also archetypal. A river might represent the flow of emotion. A house may symbolize the inner self. A locked door could point to a fear of entering a certain truth. When spirit works through dreams, they often use symbols the dreamer will understand intuitively.

Mediums can learn to speak the language of their dreams by reflecting on how each symbol made them feel rather than what it means universally. This is a subtle but powerful distinction. The emotional resonance is often more telling than the literal interpretation.

Nightmares can also carry spiritual meaning. Though they are often uncomfortable, they sometimes serve as warnings, releases, or initiations. A nightmare may reveal an energy that needs to be cleared, a suppressed memory coming to the surface, or a spirit trying to get the medium's attention.

Not all spiritual dreams are peaceful. Some are confrontational. They force the dreamer to look at what they have avoided. For the medium, this is sacred work. Shadow integration often begins in the dream world.

Some mediums experience prophetic dreams. These are dreams that seem to reveal future events or insights. While these dreams should be approached with discernment, they are often accurate and validated later.

Spirit may use dreams to prepare the medium for an upcoming situation, to offer guidance, or to help someone else through a message. The future is not always fixed, but spirit may reveal timelines, decisions, or possibilities through symbolic imagery. The key is not to become obsessed with prediction, but to use the information to support awareness, compassion, and preparedness.

Lucid dreaming is another layer of spiritual dreaming. In a lucid dream, the dreamer becomes aware that they are dreaming and can interact with the environment consciously. This state allows the medium to ask spirit direct questions, to revisit certain scenes, or to travel to different energetic dimensions.

With practice, lucid dreaming becomes a space where mediumship can be explored actively. It is a form of conscious trance that mirrors waking mediumship but within the architecture of the dream. Lucid dreams require a strong connection to the subconscious and a willingness to surrender control.

Some mediums enter dream states to meet spirit guides or to access information that is not available through waking channels. This might include past life memories, soul contracts, ancestral stories, or karmic themes.

Spirit often uses dreams to offer clarity around unresolved patterns. A dream of being chased may relate to a soul contract of avoidance. A dream of drowning could speak to a lifetime where grief was suppressed. The dream world allows for metaphor, which can bypass the ego and speak directly to the soul.

The role of sleep hygiene and physical health also plays a part in spiritual dreaming. A body that is overstimulated, exhausted, or flooded with stimulation will struggle to dream clearly. Mediums must care for their nervous systems, reduce sensory clutter, and create ritual around sleep.

This might include limiting screens before bed, using herbs or teas to calm the body, clearing the energy of the room, and setting strong intentions for dream protection. Spirit responds to intention. When the medium treats the dream space as sacred, the communication becomes more vivid.

Sleep paralysis is another phenomenon many intuitive people experience. In sleep paralysis, the body is asleep but the mind is awake. Some people report seeing shadow figures, feeling pressure, or sensing presence. While often terrifying, this state can be a powerful initiation into spiritual perception.

It is a liminal space where spirit and self-touch. Some believe this is a state where the soul is partially out of the body. Mediums who experience this can learn to protect themselves spiritually, to ground before sleep, and to call in only energies that are of love and light.

Dreams are also a place of healing. Many people receive emotional closure in dreams that they could not access in waking life. A parent may appear and say what they never could. A child may come to offer peace. A former partner may show their higher self and explain why the relationship ended the way it did. These dreams are not always literal.

They are soul dialogues. And for the medium, they offer an ongoing education in forgiveness, surrender, and the unconditional nature of spirit.

The subconscious is also where creative inspiration is born. Many mediums who are also artists, writers, or musicians receive their most powerful ideas in dreams.

This is because the soul does not see a difference between art and message. A painting can be a transmission. A song can be a channelled healing. A poem may be the voice of a guide in disguise. By honouring the dream material that seems unrelated to mediumship, the medium actually expands their channel. Spirit loves to speak through beauty.

By encouraging children to talk about their dreams, to draw them, or to keep dream journals, we preserve the soul's natural connection with the other world. This also helps the next generation of mediums grow up without shame or suppression.

Not all dreams are meant to be interpreted. Some are energetic. They reset the system, clear emotion, or allow the soul to rest in another realm. The medium must learn to trust that not every message needs to be understood. Some need only to be felt. Others may unfold weeks or years later. Spirit works in spirals, not timelines. The dream that made no sense today may be the key to tomorrow's awakening.

Mediums must also confront their resistance to dreamwork. Some avoid it out of fear of what they will see. Others believe only waking messages count. But the dream world is the original temple. It is where the ancestors spoke. It is where the veil thins without effort. In sleep, we return to source.

In dreams, we remember what we are. The medium who opens to their dreams becomes twice the channel. They carry not only the voice of spirit but the echo of soul.

To work with dreams as a medium is to become a dream walker. It is to cross thresholds nightly and return with medicine. It is to listen not just with the mind but with the body. It is to decode emotion, energy, and symbol. It is to see sleep not as escape but as a sacred appointment.

The future of mediumship includes dreaming. It includes the subconscious. It includes the soul's quiet messages in the night. It invites us to look deeper, to listen differently, and to receive even in stillness. They are portals and when the medium walks through, they bring back light for us all.

Dreams are one of the most powerful gateways to the subconscious mind and play a vital role in the development of mediumship. In the dream state, the conscious mind softens, allowing the intuitive self to come forward without resistance or logic-based filtering.

For mediums, this opens a sacred space where spirit communication can occur with clarity and symbolism, often revealing messages, unresolved energies, or ancestral presences in deeply personal ways. Paying attention to dreams, recording them, and learning their language trains the medium to recognize the subtle patterns of spirit.

The subconscious stores not only the memories of this life, but the echoes of other realms and in dreams, those echoes become the whispers of truth.

Reflection Questions: The Role of Dreams and the Subconscious in Mediumship

1. What recurring dreams or dream symbols have followed me throughout life, and what messages might they hold from spirit?

2. Have I ever received a visit or message from a spirit in a dream and how did it differ from waking communication?

3. What patterns or fears arise in my dreams that mirror blocks in my mediumship or personal healing?

4. Do I pay attention to my dreams as a sacred part of my intuitive and spiritual development?

5. How often do I explore my subconscious beliefs about death, spirit, or my own worthiness to receive?

6. What old emotional wounds still live in my subconscious and how do they affect my clarity as a medium?

7. When I dream of ancestors, past lives, or otherworldly places, how do I interpret those messages; metaphor, memory, or message?

8. How do I use dreamwork or journaling to deepen my awareness of what my inner world is trying to show me?

9. Are there any unresolved stories in my subconscious that spirit repeatedly reflects back in readings?

10. What archetypes, symbols, or images commonly appear in my dreams, and how do they align with my spiritual path?

11. Have I ever dreamed something that later came true or appeared in a reading? What did that teach me?

12. Do I create space before sleep to invite spirit or the subconscious to speak to me and how do I honour what arrives?

13. What role does the dream state play in healing parts of me that I am not yet ready to face in waking life?

14. Do I ever experience dreamlike sensations or images during readings and how do I differentiate them from imagination?

15. How can I better integrate dream messages into my conscious practice as a medium?

16. If my subconscious was a sacred mirror, what is it asking me to acknowledge, accept, or release right now?

23. Attachment Theory and the Spirit Relationship

Mediumship is not simply the transmission of messages from one realm to another. It is a deeply relational practice, rooted in the way we form bonds, hold space for others, and regulate emotional connection.

At its core, mediumship is the art of relationship. Not just with the spirits who come through, but with the living people we read for, and perhaps most importantly, with ourselves. One of the most overlooked yet transformative psychological frameworks for understanding mediumship is attachment theory.

When a medium understands their own attachment style, they begin to see how their energetic wiring impacts everything from their connection with spirit to the way they respond to clients in vulnerable states.

Attachment theory describes how early childhood relationships with caregivers shape the way we form emotional bonds later in life. These early relational patterns become internal working models; templates for how we expect love, support, and communication to unfold.

The four primary attachment styles are secure, anxious, avoidant, and disorganized. While most people carry traits from more than one category, we all tend to default to one core pattern when emotionally activated. In the context of mediumship, these patterns shape how we engage with spirit, how we process intuitive information, and how we navigate the emotional landscapes of others.

A medium with a secure attachment style is likely to feel stable in their connection to spirit. They trust the flow of information. They do not panic when a reading is unclear. They know that love from the other side is consistent and accessible. They are also able to sit with a client's emotional responses without becoming overwhelmed or dismissive.

Their relationship with their guides is balanced, not codependent. They recognize that spirit is always present, even when they themselves need rest or time away from the work. This internal security creates a strong foundation for mediumship to flourish without fear, urgency, or distortion.

In contrast, a medium with an anxious attachment style may feel a desperate need for validation from spirit. They may become overly dependent on receiving signs, synchronicities, or immediate feedback in order to feel connected. They might fear that if they are not constantly practicing, meditating, or channelling, they will lose their gift. In sessions, they may become overly invested in the client's approval, fearing that a negative reaction means they have failed.

These mediums are often incredibly empathetic and sensitive, but their inner child is often still seeking proof that they are safe, worthy, and loved. This can lead to burnout, inconsistency, and emotional exhaustion if not addressed with compassion and care.

The avoidant medium may struggle to fully surrender to the emotional vulnerability that mediumship requires. They might downplay the emotional content of spirit messages or remain overly analytical in their readings. They may feel discomfort when clients cry, or detach from their own grief in order to appear professional or composed.

This pattern can also show up in the medium's relationship with spirit. They may receive clear messages but resist integrating them into their personal life. They might dismiss emotional prompts from their guides or avoid deeper spiritual intimacy. Underneath the detachment is often a fear of being overwhelmed, abandoned, or not in control. Avoidant mediums benefit from learning to feel safe in emotional closeness, both with spirit and with themselves.

Disorganized attachment, also known as fearful avoidant, is marked by a push-pull dynamic.

Mediums with this pattern may deeply crave spiritual connection but fear the vulnerability it brings. They may swing between hyper-spiritual intensity and complete withdrawal. In readings, they may struggle with inconsistency, self-doubt, or overwhelm. They may receive profound insights but then question their sanity or worthiness. Their relationship with spirit may feel chaotic, as if they are unsure whether they are being supported or tested.

This attachment style often arises from trauma, and healing it requires deep inner work, nervous system regulation, and compassionate support from mentors or therapists.

Understanding one's attachment style is not about labelling or limiting oneself. It is about creating awareness. When a medium knows their patterns, they can recognize when fear is driving their choices rather than trust. They can pause, self-regulate, and reorient toward connection rather than control.

Attachment work invites the medium to reparent themselves, to create safety within their own body and psyche, and to offer that safety to others in the reading space. Spirit work cannot bypass human need. It must include it. The way we bond in life often mirrors the way we bond in spirit.

Clients also bring their attachment styles into readings. An anxious client may need reassurance, repeated validation, or emotional holding. An avoidant client may resist vulnerable messages or downplay their own feelings. A disorganized client may crave connection but distrust the entire experience. A securely attached client may be more open, trusting, and grounded.

Understanding this allows the medium to meet clients where they are, without judgment or frustration. It also helps the medium avoid personalizing the client's reactions. Not every tear is a reflection of the reading's success. Not every shutdown is a reflection of failure. People receive spirit messages through the lens of their own nervous systems.

Spirit guides often work to repair or reflect attachment wounds. For example, a client who never felt seen by their father may receive a message from him in spirit that says exactly what they longed to hear. A client with a history of abandonment may hear from a grandparent who affirms that they were always there, even if unseen.

These messages do not erase the past, but they can begin to shift the internal working model. The medium becomes a witness to this repair. They do not force it. They hold space for it. This is why mediumship is not simply about delivering facts. It is about offering presence in a moment of transformation.

The medium's relationship with their own guides is also shaped by attachment dynamics. Some mediums speak of their guides as parental figures, siblings, or close friends. Others relate to them as abstract energies or higher aspects of themselves.

A medium with unresolved attachment wounds may unconsciously project those dynamics onto their guides. They may fear being abandoned if they do not practice enough. They may feel punished when messages are unclear. They may idolize the guide and lose their own sense of autonomy.

Recognizing these patterns allows the medium to step into a more balanced and conscious relationship with the spirit team. Guides are not there to dominate. They are there to partner.

Mediumship training should include some understanding of attachment theory. It is not enough to teach mechanics and technique. Students must learn to understand their emotional blueprint. They must become aware of when their inner child is seeking validation through spirit. They must be able to regulate themselves when a session stirs grief, fear, or shame.

A strong medium is not one who is always accurate. A strong medium is one who can stay connected to themselves in the presence of another's pain. This begins with attachment repair.

Practices that support secure attachment include inner child work, nervous system regulation, somatic healing, and compassionate witnessing. A medium might ask their younger self, "What do you need from spirit today?" or "How can I help you feel safe while we open to this energy?"

This internal dialogue creates safety. It makes the body a safe place for spirit to land. It also ensures that the messages are not filtered through trauma, projection, or unmet need. When the inner child feels held, the adult self becomes more available to receive truth.

Attachment healing also opens the door to deeper trust. Mediums who have done this work often speak of a felt sense of being held by spirit. They are less afraid of being wrong. They are more open to silence. They do not panic when a message takes time to come through. They trust the relationship with spirit as much as the information.

This trust radiates into their client relationships. Clients feel safe because the medium is not reactive, insecure, or performative. They are steady. They are present. They are attuned.

The collective healing of attachment wounds is deeply spiritual. Many of the world's challenges stem from disconnection, fear of abandonment, and the loss of secure relational bonds. Mediumship, when practiced with emotional intelligence, becomes part of the remedy. It reminds people that they are still connected, still loved, still seen. It offers an experience of attuned presence, even if only for an hour. That hour can shift a lifetime.

In many ways, spirit speaks in the language of secure attachment. Their messages are consistent, kind, and validating. They often reflect the opposite of what the person experienced in life. This contrast is healing. It gives the soul a new template. A new story. And the medium is the bridge for that transmission.

To deepen in this work, the medium can ask themselves: How do I respond when I feel disconnected from spirit? Do I panic or trust? Do I chase signs or rest in presence? How do I respond when a client becomes emotional or shuts down? Do I lean in or pull away? How do I care for my own inner emotional needs before and after readings? Do I believe I am worthy of being supported by spirit even when I am not perfect?

These questions open the door to growth, stability, and freedom in the channel.

Ultimately, mediumship is not separate from human psychology. It is shaped by it, expressed through it, and matured by it. Attachment theory offers a compassionate lens through which to understand the medium's sensitivity, vulnerability, and power.

It reminds us that spirit connection is not just a skill. It is a relationship. And like any relationship, it flourishes when we feel safe, seen, and worthy. The more the medium heals their own attachment wounds, the more clearly they can mirror love for others.

Not just through the words they speak, but through the way they listen, hold space, and allow love to move through them.

In the spirit world, attachments are more than emotional bonds; they are energetic threads that weave through time, connecting us to those we have loved, grieved, and promised to find again.

For the medium, understanding attachment becomes a path to deeper compassion, recognizing that the desperate need to connect with the departed often mirrors the wounded child within who once reached for love and feared abandonment. Spirit does not exploit these attachments but gently meets them, teaching us through presence and grace that true connection is never severed, only transformed.

In healing our attachments, we don't learn to let go of love, we learn to love more freely, beyond fear, beyond form, and beyond death.

24. Inner Archetypes and the Medium's Soul Role

Within every medium lives a constellation of archetypes, ancient patterns of energy, behaviour, and essence that shape the way their soul expresses its purpose. Archetypes are not invented by the mind. They are remembered by the soul. They are the deep symbols of who we are, etched across centuries of incarnation, mirrored in myth, dream, and collective story.

For the medium, these inner archetypes are not merely ideas. They are doorways into power, limitation, memory, and identity. Understanding the archetypes we carry helps us refine our spiritual purpose and awaken our true role as a soul-born messenger between worlds.

Carl Jung described archetypes as universal templates that live in the collective unconscious. He observed them in myths, dreams, and patterns of behaviour that repeated across time and culture. The Mother, the Warrior, the Sage, the Trickster, and the Healer are all examples.

But for the medium, there are specific archetypes that seem to appear again and again; The Seer, The Oracle, The Messenger, The Wounded Healer, The Guide, The Mystic, The Shadow Walker. These are not identities to wear. They are soul roles to embody. They shape the way we receive, transmit, and carry the energy of spirit through our unique human form.

The Seer archetype is one of the oldest roles in human history. The Seer does not merely observe. They sense the subtle realms beneath what is visible. They receive premonitions, dream symbols, emotional truths, and the unspoken stories that shape lives. In ancient cultures, the Seer was called to advise, to guide, to reveal. Their role was sacred and often feared.

In a modern context, the Seer is the intuitive who feels energy before words are spoken, who dreams of events before they unfold, who can read a room without needing explanation. The Seer medium carries an inner compass that points to hidden truths. But without grounding, the Seer can become overwhelmed, isolated, or lost in other people's stories. This archetype asks the medium to honour sensitivity as strength while cultivating strong boundaries and discernment.

The Oracle archetype carries the voice of the divine. While the Seer perceives, the Oracle speaks. Oracles often work through trance, altered states, or spontaneous downloads. Their messages are poetic, timeless, and often mysterious. In ancient temples, Oracles were vessels through which the gods would speak. They were not consulted for casual questions. Their presence demanded reverence.

Today, the Oracle medium may receive sudden bursts of wisdom that do not belong to the rational mind. They may find themselves speaking in ways that surprise even them. This archetype requires surrender. The Oracle must move past the ego's desire to control or interpret.

They must become a hollow bone through which higher truth moves. But if ungrounded, the Oracle may struggle with disassociation or lose touch with the human experience. Their path is one of balance between heaven and earth.

The Messenger is the bridge between worlds. They translate energy into language. Unlike the Oracle, who channels transcendent truth, the Messenger medium works closely with spirits of the departed. They carry specific information, memories, emotions, and validations.

Their role is one of service, delivering healing words from those who have crossed over to those who are grieving. The Messenger must be precise, ethical, and emotionally present. Their archetype is one of great compassion. They often feel called to this work after experiencing personal loss. If not careful, they may become overly identified with their gift, tying their worth to their accuracy.

The Messenger must remember that they are the vessel, not the source. Their power lies in humility.

The Wounded Healer is an archetype that many mediums unconsciously carry. Originating from the myth of Chiron, the Wounded Healer is one who has suffered deeply and uses that suffering to guide others. Their pain becomes their medicine.

Mediums with this archetype have often experienced trauma, illness, loss, or abandonment. They have walked through darkness and returned with light. They are not perfect or healed in a traditional sense. Rather, they have accepted their wounds as sacred. This archetype brings deep empathy but can also lead to burnout if the healer does not tend to their own needs.

The Wounded Healer must learn that they are not responsible for saving everyone. Their job is to hold space, to witness, and to walk beside.

The Guide archetype is the wise one. Often older in soul age, the Guide medium carries a sense of timeless knowing. They attract others who seek mentorship, teaching, or counsel.

This archetype may emerge later in a medium's journey, once they have integrated their own lessons and feel called to pass on their wisdom. The Guide is not attached to being seen. They are often quiet, observing, and listening. When they speak, it is with clarity and depth. Their challenge is to remain in integrity, to avoid power dynamics, and to continually empty themselves so that spirit may move through them anew. The Guide walks with both confidence and humility.

The Mystic is the medium who sees all life as sacred. They are less interested in proof and more interested in presence. They feel the divine in all things, in trees, in breath, in silence, in suffering. The Mystic medium may find themselves drawn to solitude, nature, or contemplative practices. They often speak in symbols, feel deeply, and perceive reality as layered and multi-dimensional. Their challenge is to remain anchored in the body. Mystics may become ungrounded or feel disconnected from everyday life.

Their medicine is to root their vision in the here and now, to translate the infinite into the intimate.

The Shadow Walker is the medium who does not fear the dark. They are drawn to the edges of grief, trauma, and suffering. They often help spirits who are restless, lost, or burdened. They may work in haunted spaces, navigate psychic attack, or guide clients through the release of ancestral pain.

The Shadow Walker knows that light cannot exist without darkness. They are initiates in the sacred art of transmutation. Their presence brings depth and transformation. But they must be careful not to become consumed by what they witness. This archetype requires strong energetic hygiene, self-awareness, and spiritual protection. It is not an easy path, but it is a holy one.

Most mediums carry more than one archetype. Some carry three or four that blend and shift over time. What matters is not which archetype one identifies with most, but how consciously one lives it. These archetypes are not boxes. They are mirrors. They show us what energies move through us most strongly. They show us what we are here to remember, embody, and offer.

A medium who knows their archetypal patterns can better understand their triggers, strengths, fears, and gifts.

Archetypes can also shift as we evolve. A medium may begin as a Wounded Healer, drawn to the work by their own pain. As they grow, they may step into the role of the Guide or the Oracle. These shifts are natural. They reflect the soul's unfolding. Mediumship is not a static identity. It is a living path. By tracking which archetypes are present at different stages, the medium can honour their own evolution.

The archetypal lens also helps the medium understand the spirits they connect with. Spirit often shows up in archetypal form. A grandmother who appears in a dream may carry the essence of the Great Mother. A soldier who visits a haunted battlefield may embody the Wounded Warrior. A spirit guide may speak in the voice of the Sage. These are not tricks of the mind. They are symbolic expressions that allow spirit to communicate more clearly.

When the medium understands archetypal language, they can interpret messages more deeply.

Archetypes are also cultural. They are shaped by the stories, myths, and symbols we grow up with. A Celtic medium may resonate with the archetype of the Bard or the Druid. An Indigenous medium may carry the energy of the Dream walker or the Medicine Person. Archetypes are universal in form but personal in expression.

This is why it is so important to honour the cultural roots of the archetypes we work with. Appropriation distorts energy. Reverence restores it.

Meditation and journey work can help a medium discover their core archetypes.

In stillness, one can ask, "What archetype is most alive in me now?" or "What soul role am I being asked to embody at this time?" The answers often come in images, feelings, or symbols. A sword may signify the Warrior. A mirror may reveal the Seer. A flame may represent the Mystic. These symbols speak the language of the soul. They are not to be rushed or decoded too quickly. They are to be lived with, danced with, and explored over time.

Understanding one's soul role is not about creating identity. It is about aligning with purpose. When a medium honours their archetypal path, they move with more clarity and compassion. They stop comparing themselves to others. They stop chasing someone else's version of success. They know who they are, and they know why they are here. This knowing creates depth in their work. It creates peace in their practice. It creates space for spirit to move freely.

There is great freedom in archetypal awareness. It allows the medium to let go of perfection, of pressure, of performance. It invites them into presence. It reminds them that they are not the first to walk this path, nor will they be the last. They are part of an ancient lineage. They are walking with ancestors, with stories, with symbols that have always existed. The archetypes live within. They are not separate. They are soul memory returning.

In the end, the soul role of the medium is unique to each individual.

No two Seers are the same. No two Mystics speak alike. What matters is that the medium honours the shape of their own soul. That they trust their inner design. That they let the archetypes rise not as masks but as guides.

When this happens, mediumship becomes not just a skill, but a sacred remembering.

The medium becomes not just a communicator, but a living archetype themselves, a walking bridge between the world of form and the world of essence, and in that walk, healing happens. Truth awakens. Spirit speaks.

Understanding and accepting your mediumship archetype is a sacred act of self-recognition, a return to the spiritual blueprint that your soul chose long before this lifetime.

Each medium carries a unique energetic signature; some are seers, others are healers, messengers, shadow walkers, or bridge keepers between realms. Your archetype is not a label to restrict you but a mirror to reflect the deeper truth of how your gift wishes to be expressed. When you understand your archetype, you stop comparing your path to others and begin honouring your own rhythm, style, and purpose.

Acceptance brings alignment. It helps you discern when to serve, when to rest, and how to nurture your abilities in ways that resonate with your soul rather than external expectation. In embracing your archetype, you step into your mediumship not as a role, but as a remembrance of who you have always been.

Reflection Questions: Inner Archetypes and the Medium's Soul Role

1. What archetypes do I naturally embody in my spiritual work, the healer, the messenger, the seer, the priestess, the wounded child?

2. How do these inner archetypes shape the way I deliver messages, hold space, and connect with spirit?

3. Which parts of me feel ancient, as though they have been doing this work across lifetimes?

4. Are there archetypes within me that feel overdeveloped or exhausted and others that are asking to rise and be reclaimed?

5. When I step into a reading, which version of myself shows up first: the guide, the protector, the nurturer, the truth-teller?

6. What soul contract or sacred vow do I feel I made before this life that continues to guide my work as a medium?

7. How do the wounds of my inner archetypes influence the type of spirits or messages I tend to attract?

8. What forgotten or rejected parts of me are actually holding keys to my most powerful, authentic form of mediumship?

9. Am I willing to evolve past an old archetype, one that kept me safe or defined for the sake of deeper spiritual truth?

10. If I could name the soul role I came here to fulfill through mediumship, what would I call it and why?

11. What archetypes do I resist or fear becoming, and could those hold hidden aspects of my power or truth?

12. How does my dominant archetype react under pressure, self-doubt, or spiritual exhaustion and what does that teach me about balance?

13. In moments of deep alignment with spirit, what archetype do I feel fully embodied and how can I honour that part of me more often in daily life?

14. How do my archetypes evolve over time, what parts of me are dying, being reborn, or stepping into new spiritual leadership?

15. If spirit were to name the archetype I am currently living through, what would it be and what lesson is it asking me to master?

16. What would it mean to live in full alignment with my soul's archetype, not just in my mediumship, but in every part of my life?

25. Cultural and Cross-Spiritual Mediumship

Mediumship is not confined to one belief system, one country, or one historical moment. It is a universal human experience that has emerged in every culture across time. From the oracle temples of ancient Greece to the trance healers of the Amazon rainforest, from the ancestral altars of West Africa to the whispering seiðr of the Norse shamans, the impulse to speak with the unseen, to bridge the visible and the invisible, is embedded in the fabric of human consciousness.

Yet in the modern spiritual world, mediumship is often presented through a narrow Western lens, one that risks erasing the rich diversity of how spirit communication is expressed, understood, and honoured globally. To be a conscious and ethical medium today is to begin unlearning this limitation and to open to the beauty of cultural and cross-spiritual awareness.

The truth is, every culture has its own language for what we call mediumship. Some cultures refer to it as spirit possession, others as ancestral communion, others as divine revelation, prophecy, oracle work, or trance healing. The words change, but the essence remains.

The medium is the vessel, the in-between, the human threshold through which non-ordinary knowledge comes forth. This makes the medium not just a practitioner of a technique, but a cultural translator of energy, meaning, and healing. And just as language differs between cultures, so too does the role, the training, the ethics, and the purpose of the medium.

In many Indigenous cultures, the role of the medium is not chosen by the individual but by the community or by spirit itself. A person might begin experiencing illness, visions, or altered states that indicate they are being called to serve. These initiations are not always gentle.

Often, they involve suffering, separation, and years of training. In the Dagara tradition of Burkina Faso, for example, spiritual illness is a sign that a person is being summoned by the ancestors to fulfill a healing role.

The community does not pathologize these experiences. Instead, they guide the individual through ritual, apprenticeship, and ancestral connection. This view stands in stark contrast to the Western tendency to medicalize or suppress spiritual emergence.

By honouring cultural frameworks for spirit calling, we expand our understanding of what it means to become a medium.

In Afro-Caribbean traditions such as Vodou, Candomblé, and Santería, mediumship often involves possession by deities or spirits known as orishas, lwa, or egun. These spiritual beings enter the body during sacred ritual and speak through the medium to offer guidance, blessings, or healing. The medium in these traditions is not simply relaying messages from a distance. They are temporarily inhabited by the divine.

This form of spirit embodiment requires rigorous training, spiritual cleanliness, and deep trust in the community structure. It is not entered lightly. The medium becomes the living altar, a sacred conduit for divine intelligence. When viewed through this lens, mediumship is not just a personal skill but a collective ceremony.

The medium's body is not theirs alone. It belongs to spirit and to the people.

Across Asia, mediumship expresses itself through temple trance practices, ancestral shrines, and Buddhist channelled states. In Taiwan, spirit mediums known as tang-ki enter deep trance to communicate with local gods or ancestors. These messages are often delivered during public festivals and include both divination and spiritual healing.

In India, certain forms of possession mediumship appear in village traditions where deities are invoked into the body for specific periods. These moments are culturally understood, contextualized, and respected. The role of the medium is often hereditary, passed down through generations, and supported by strong ritual frameworks. Again, we see that mediumship is not simply about individual intuition. It is embedded within the lineage, the landscape, and the community memory.

In Indigenous Australian spirituality, the ancestral realm is deeply present in everyday life. The Dreaming, an ongoing spiritual reality that holds ancestral wisdom and creation energy is not past, but ever-living.

While not described as mediumship in the Western sense, communication with ancestors, spirits, and the land itself is central. Elders, songlines, and ceremony all play a part in maintaining these spiritual relationships.

The medium in this context is not a separate person but a role fulfilled by those chosen by country and story. This understanding reminds us that spirit communication is not always about speaking with the dead. It can also be about listening to the earth, to animals, to winds, and to sacred space. It is about attunement, not dominance.

When modern Western mediums ignore or appropriate these traditions, harm is done. Mediumship does not exist in a vacuum. It is shaped by colonial histories, religious suppression, and systems of power.

Many of the spiritual systems now celebrated in wellness spaces were once criminalized or erased. To practice mediumship today without acknowledging these histories is to perpetuate the very systems that once silenced the ancestors we now claim to hear. Cultural awareness is not optional for the ethical medium. It is a responsibility. It is a form of reverence. It requires listening, humility, and willingness to de-centre oneself.

Cross-spiritual awareness means the medium recognizes that spirit does not belong to any one religion or system. Spirit is not Christian or Pagan or Buddhist. Spirit is spirit. But people are shaped by their traditions, beliefs, and spiritual languages. When a spirit comes through in a reading, they often use imagery or symbols familiar to the sitter. A Christian client may receive messages through angels or saints.

A Wiccan client may experience the spirit as a guide in the form of an animal or element. A Buddhist sitter may describe messages as visions or light experiences. The medium must learn to speak in many languages. Not of words, but of meaning. To translate energy in a way that honours the worldview of the person receiving it.

This does not mean the medium must study every religion in detail. But it does mean being open, respectful, and curious. It means not assuming that spirit only speaks through one framework. It means understanding that the veil looks different depending on who is looking through it. The medium is not just a receiver of messages.

They are an interpreter. And every interpreter must understand context.

One of the greatest dangers in cross-spiritual mediumship is spiritual appropriation. This occurs when a medium takes rituals, symbols, or titles from a culture not their own without understanding, permission, or respect. For example, referring to oneself as a shaman without lineage or community recognition can be deeply harmful.

Using sacred tools from Indigenous cultures without proper training or relationship can desecrate rather than honour. The medium must ask: Am I using this because it feels powerful, or because I have been invited into a relationship with it? Relationship is the key. Spirit work is not transactional. It is relational. And relationships require reciprocity.

That said, spirit often calls people across cultural lines. A medium may feel a strong connection to a tradition they were not born into. If this happens, the path forward is one of humility, education, and reverence. It involves finding teachers within that tradition, listening to elders, and being in right relationship with the land, people, and practices involved.

Spirit will never ask a medium to dishonour another culture. True guidance always includes integrity.

The concept of soul memory complicates this further. Many mediums remember past lives in different cultures. They may feel drawn to traditions that once belonged to them but no longer do in this lifetime. This is not wrong, but it must be navigated with care. A soul may carry memory from an African priesthood, a Norse seiðr tradition, or an Egyptian temple.

But the medium must also honour the reality of their current lifetime. Past life memory is a gift, not a license. It is meant to enrich, not to bypass present-day accountability.

The medium must also be mindful of how trauma shows up across cultures. For some clients, their relationship with spirit is shaped by religious wounding, colonization, or generational silence. A person who grew up in a strict religious household may carry fear around mediumship, even as they seek it out.

A client from a culture where mediumship was demonized or forbidden may carry shame, confusion, or ancestral resistance. The medium must hold these layers with tenderness. Spirit is not just delivering messages. Spirit is also healing these fractures.

Cultural grief is also a powerful force. Many people feel disconnected from their ancestral traditions due to forced assimilation, displacement, or diaspora. In these cases, mediumship can offer a path of reconnection. Spirit may come through with ancestral practices, names, or symbols that the client never knew consciously.

The role of the medium here is not to teach the tradition but to create space for the client's own remembering. The messages become not just communication but restoration. The spirit world becomes a place of cultural return.

Cross-spiritual mediumship also invites us to explore how different traditions view death itself. In the West, death is often medicalized, feared, and sanitized. In other cultures, death is communal, sacred, and participatory. In Mexico, Día de los Muertos is a vibrant celebration of the ancestors. In Bali, cremation ceremonies are elaborate communal rites. In Tibetan Buddhism, the Bardo teachings describe the soul's journey through various realms.

When a medium works with spirits from different cultural backgrounds, they must consider how those spirits experienced death and how they may wish to be honoured. A spirit who was part of a culture that reveres ancestor worship may seek offerings or ritual acknowledgment. The medium who is sensitive to these differences creates a more accurate and respectful connection.

Mediumship training in the future must include cultural awareness as a core component. This does not mean tokenism or superficial nods to diversity. It means learning about the global history of spirit communication, understanding colonial impacts on spirituality, and cultivating relationships with teachers from diverse backgrounds.

It means asking hard questions, listening deeply, and being willing to be corrected. True spiritual growth includes cultural humility.

In the end, cross-spiritual mediumship is not about collecting traditions. It is about becoming a vessel spacious enough to hold many truths. It is about remembering that spirit does not care what language we use but does care how we use it. It is about honouring the ancestors of the land we live on and the ancestors of the land we came from. It is about healing not only the individual but the collective.

The medium who walks this path does not walk alone.

They walk with the spirits of many nations, the songs of many lands, and the prayers of many tongues. Their gift is not ownership. It is devotion. And in that devotion, they become the bridge, not just between worlds, but between cultures, wounds, and possibilities. They become a voice not just for the dead, but for the memory of how beautifully alive humanity once was when spirit was honoured in every corner of the earth.

26. Dissociation or Trance? Psychological Risks and Spiritual Truths

Mediumship often involves entering altered states of consciousness to receive, translate, or deliver messages from the spirit world. These states range from soft intuitive openness to deep trance, where the medium's awareness may step aside entirely to allow another consciousness to speak.

For many, this is one of the most mysterious and beautiful aspects of mediumship. It is the point at which the veil truly thins and the self becomes a bridge. Yet within this territory lies a delicate psychological landscape. Not every altered state is sacred. Not every detachment is spiritual.

At times, what appears to be a trance state may actually be dissociation, a survival mechanism rooted in trauma rather than transformation. Understanding the difference between trance and dissociation is essential not only for the health of the medium but for the integrity of their work.

Dissociation is the mind's way of escaping overwhelming stress, fear, or pain. It is a psychological defence that allows a person to detach from the present moment when it becomes too much to bear. This detachment can take many forms: a sense of being outside one's body, a numbing of emotion, a feeling that time is not real, or a sense that the world is dreamlike or unreal.

Dissociation can be mild or severe, momentary or chronic. In trauma survivors, especially those with complex post-traumatic stress, dissociation often develops early in life as a necessary survival strategy. It is not a weakness. It is the nervous system's attempt to protect itself from unbearable reality.

Trance, on the other hand, is a conscious surrender into a different state of awareness. It is a sacred descent, an intentional shift, often accompanied by ritual, breath, or deep meditative focus. In trance, the medium may feel their sense of identity soften or step aside, but the experience is rooted in presence, not avoidance.

There is a sense of being connected to something greater, not escaping from something unbearable. Trance is not numbing. It is deepening. The trance state is a tool, a vessel, a spiritual technology. It may look like dissociation from the outside, but on the inside, it feels entirely different. The body remains a sacred container. The soul remains engaged.

For mediums who have a history of trauma, however, the line between trance and dissociation can blur. What feels like a spiritual state may in fact be the nervous system shutting down. What appears to be channelling may be an unprocessed split of identity.

This is not a judgment. It is a reality that many spiritual practitioners face. It is not uncommon for highly intuitive individuals to have traumatic backgrounds. The sensitivity that allows one to sense spirit can also be born from a childhood of hypervigilance, emotional neglect, or abuse.

Many mediums were once children who had to read the energy of a room before walking into it. That ability, while later spiritualized, was first a form of survival.

This is why psychological education is essential in mediumship training. Mediums must learn to recognize the signs of dissociation in themselves and others. They must be able to differentiate between a healthy spiritual surrender and an unconscious shutdown.

For example, if a medium often forgets what happened during a session and has no memory of what was said, that may be trance, or it may be a form of dissociation known as amnesia. If the medium leaves their body frequently and cannot ground back into the present moment, that may not be spirit. It may be an old trauma pattern repeating itself under the guise of sacred work.

Grounding is one of the most reliable indicators. After a genuine trance experience, the medium may feel altered but still able to return. There is a soft landing. There is integration.

After dissociation, the return may be jarring, confusing, or emotionally overwhelming. The body may feel foreign. There may be shame, fatigue, or disconnection. In trance, the channel feels purposeful. In dissociation, the split feels protective. The intention behind the shift matters. Intention is what separates a sacred state from a survival mechanism.

Another indicator is emotional clarity. After a trance state, the medium often feels expanded, connected, even if the session was difficult. There is a spiritual coherence. After dissociation, the medium may feel foggy, detached, or numb. The emotions may not make sense. There may be gaps in memory or a sense of having vanished. Trance deepens access to truth. Dissociation suppresses it.

Trance invites the medium to embody more of who they are. Dissociation invites the medium to forget.

The medium's relationship with their own nervous system is critical. Learning somatic tools, trauma-informed mindfulness, and emotional regulation helps the medium build a strong foundation. A regulated body is the safest place for spirit to land. If the body is constantly in fight, flight, or freeze, the messages that come through may be distorted or disconnected. Spirit does not need perfection.

But spirit does need presence. A medium who is grounded in their own body can offer clearer, safer, and more consistent communication.

This is not to say that trance cannot feel intense. At times, it may involve trembling, crying, or a sense of being profoundly moved. But there is a thread of connection that runs through it. The medium is not lost. They are held.

Spirit often anchors them in this altered state, ensuring they do not fall into overwhelm. But if the medium has not built that inner anchor, they may unconsciously use trance states as a way to escape life.

This becomes spiritual bypassing, the use of spiritual practices to avoid dealing with emotional pain or trauma. A medium may become addicted to being in altered states, avoiding the discomfort of everyday life, relationships, or unresolved wounds.

The danger here is not just personal. It affects clients as well. A medium who channels from a dissociated state may deliver information that is disconnected, fragmented, or lacking emotional resonance. They may appear distant, robotic, or overly theatrical.

The client may leave the session feeling confused or unseen. Worse, if the medium is projecting unprocessed trauma into the session, the client may receive messages that carry subtle fear, shame, or judgment. The sacred space becomes clouded by unconscious pain.

This is why supervision, mentorship, and therapy are essential parts of the medium's journey. Just as therapists require clinical supervision to ensure they are not bringing their personal wounds into the therapy room, so too should mediums seek guidance and reflection. Spiritual development is not a substitute for psychological integration.

Both are needed. The more the medium understands their own psyche, the more clearly they can serve.

It is also important to acknowledge that trauma and spiritual awakening can coexist.

Many mediums go through a period of awakening that stirs deep emotional pain.

Memories may surface. Old wounds may reopen. The soul may be calling them to clear what has been buried. This is not a sign of regression. It is a sacred unravelling. But it must be held carefully. Without support, the medium may mistake trauma activation for spiritual ascension. They may believe their suffering is a sign of higher calling, rather than a call to healing.

Spirit will never ask a medium to bypass their own healing. In fact, spirit often refuses to deepen the channel until the medium has done their inner work.

Safe trance work begins with preparation. The body must feel safe. The nervous system must be regulated. The space must be protected. The intention must be clear. The medium must be resourced enough to return.

Practices such as breathwork, grounding visualizations, and post-trance integration rituals help create this container. Mediums must also learn when not to go into trance. If they are emotionally depleted, physically ill, or spiritually unclear, it is better to pause. Spirit will always honour the medium's boundaries. Spirit prefers a present channel to a fractured one.

Trance work can also be sacredly initiated. In many cultures, entering trance is not a casual occurrence. It is preceded by prayer, fasting, or ceremonial preparation. The community holds space. The spirits are invoked with reverence. The body is treated as temple. This context matters. It teaches the medium that altered states are not entertainment. They are offerings.

They are acts of surrender that require maturity, integrity, and support. Without this framework, trance work can become exploitative or unsafe.

For mediums who have experienced dissociation, healing is possible. The body can relearn safety. The soul can re-inhabit the form. With trauma-informed care, the medium can begin to tell the difference between a shutdown and a surrender. They can learn to stay with themselves during intense experiences. They can root into the earth while reaching toward the heavens. This embodiment creates a clearer, safer channel. Spirit always meets us where we are.

When we commit to healing, spirit deepens the bond.

The medium who understands this territory becomes a guide not only between worlds, but within worlds. They are able to walk others through their own fragmentation. They are able to say, with honesty and compassion, I know what it feels like to leave yourself. And I also know the way home. Their presence becomes medicine. Not because they have escaped pain, but because they have befriended it. They are not afraid of the dark.

They have walked through it with a lamp in hand.

In the end, the difference between trance and dissociation is not always visible to the outside world. But to the medium, it is everything. It is the difference between presence and absence, connection and escape, truth and distortion. The work of a conscious medium is to remain in relationship with spirit, with clients, with self. That relationship is the channel. It is not built in the heavens. It is built in the body. When the body is safe, the soul can speak. When the soul speaks, spirit answers and when spirit answers, healing begins.

Reflection Questions: Dissociation or Trance?

1. When I enter a trance-like state during mediumship, do I feel safe, present, and grounded or numb, disconnected, and disoriented?

2. How do I distinguish between a healthy altered state of spiritual attunement and psychological dissociation triggered by unresolved trauma?

3. What emotional or physical signs does my body give me when I am moving out of alignment and into escapism?

4. Have I ever used trance as a way to avoid uncomfortable feelings, personal issues, or human vulnerability?

5. What practices or grounding rituals help me return fully to my body after working in expanded states of consciousness?

6. Am I willing to examine my trance practices with honesty, humility, and curiosity to ensure they are both spiritually aligned and psychologically safe?

27. The Witch Wound and the Medium's Inherited Fear

There is a silence that echoes through the bones of many spiritual practitioners. It is not the silence of doubt or lack of belief. It is the silence of suppression, inherited through generations, passed down like a secret warning.

It whispers, do not speak too loudly. Do not be too visible. Do not be too powerful. This silence is the witch wound. It is the inherited trauma that many mediums, healers, and intuitive beings carry in their nervous systems, bloodlines, and memories. It does not always speak in words, but it shows up in how we hide, in how we second-guess our truth, in how we shrink back from our own gifts.

To be a medium in the modern world is to reckon with this ancient wound and to decide, again and again, that we will no longer carry the weight of silence.

The witch wound is not just a metaphor. It is a real psychological and spiritual imprint created through centuries of persecution, punishment, and patriarchal control of intuitive and spiritual power.

Across Europe, the Americas, and beyond, people, especially women and feminine-presenting individuals were accused of witchcraft and subjected to torture, execution, exile, or public humiliation. These accusations were often not about magic at all.

They were about power, land, medicine, sexuality, and the fear of feminine wisdom. Herbalists, midwives, oracles, and spiritual leaders were targeted under religious and political systems that sought to dominate the body and the soul. The trauma inflicted was not only individual. It was collective. Families were broken. Communities were turned against one another. Entire lineages of wisdom were cut down.

Mediums are among the most direct inheritors of this wound. We speak with the dead. We hear voices that others do not hear. We are often deeply sensitive, intuitive, and tuned into energies that society has long tried to deny.

Many of us have experienced fear not just in this life, but as a memory from other lifetimes, memories of being burned, drowned, betrayed, silenced, or cast out. These are not simply stories. They are soul imprints. The body remembers what the mind has forgotten. And when we step into the work of mediumship, we awaken those memories. We stir the ashes. We unearth the bones. We reclaim what was taken.

This reclamation is not easy. The witch wound often shows up in modern mediums as anxiety, imposter syndrome, chronic self-doubt, or an unexplained fear of being seen. It whispers that we are not safe to be public with our gifts. It warns us that others will turn on us, laugh at us, or call us dangerous. These fears are not always irrational. They are echoes of real historical trauma.

Even today, mediums may be ridiculed, banned from spiritual spaces, or misunderstood by their families and peers. The fear of persecution may live quietly in the background of every reading, every message, every post we make.

We ask ourselves, who am I to do this? What if they come for me?

To move beyond the witch wound, we must first name it. We must acknowledge that many of the psychological struggles mediums face are not simply personal—they are ancestral. They are inherited. They are systemic and they are not shameful. They are sacred. They are the evidence that we are healing a very old story. The moment we step forward and say, I am a medium, we are rewriting that story. We are saying that truth is more powerful than fear. We are saying that connection is stronger than control.

Healing the witch wound requires both inner and outer work. Internally, the medium must begin to develop safety in the body. When the nervous system has been shaped by generations of fear, it takes time to rewire.

Practices such as breathwork, grounding, somatic awareness, and trauma-informed therapy help to reestablish the feeling of safety. When the body feels safe, the soul can step forward. The medium can begin to feel the difference between actual danger and inherited fear. They can begin to speak not from panic, but from power.

Shadow work is another essential part of healing. The witch wound is deeply tied to shame. Shame about being different, shame about being powerful, shame about wanting to be seen.

Mediums must face the parts of themselves that still believe they are too much or not enough. They must confront the voice that says, If they see who I really am, they will leave me. This voice often comes from early life experiences, cultural conditioning, or past life trauma. It must be met with compassion, not judgment. The shadow does not need to be destroyed. It needs to be held.

Only then can the medium reclaim the full range of their expression.

On the spiritual level, the medium can work directly with ancestors who carried the witch wound. These may be family members, spiritual guides, or collective archetypes.

Through ritual, meditation, or prayer, the medium can invite these ancestors into healing. They can ask for their wisdom. They can speak the words that were never spoken. They can light candles for the women who were silenced, the men who were punished for being intuitive, the children who saw spirits and were told to hush.

In doing so, they restore the lineage. They say, the chain ends with me. I will not carry your shame. I will carry your strength.

Community is also a vital part of healing the witch wound. Persecution thrives in isolation. Connection is the antidote.

Mediums need other mediums. We need circles, mentorships, sisterhoods, and sacred gatherings where our gifts are normalized and celebrated. We need spaces where we can say, I feel scared, and not be dismissed.

Where we can say, I feel powerful, and not be shamed. The witch wound loses its grip when we stop hiding. When we are witnessed in our truth, we are healed in ways that solitude cannot offer.

Another part of healing involves redefining what it means to be powerful. The witch wound taught us that power is dangerous, corrupt, or forbidden. But true power is love in motion. It is presence. It is integrity. It is the willingness to speak truth even when the voice shakes.

Power is not domination. It is devotion. It is the ability to channel something greater than the self while remaining rooted in self. The medium who embodies true power becomes a light that no system can extinguish.

There is also a gendered aspect to the witch wound that must be addressed. While people of all genders were persecuted under witchcraft laws, women were disproportionately targeted.

Today, women and femme-presenting mediums may still face patriarchal scrutiny when they step into leadership, visibility, or spiritual authority. They may be called emotional, irrational, or delusional. These judgments are modern echoes of ancient fear. The feminine has long been associated with mystery, emotion, intuition, and the body, all things that patriarchal systems have tried to control. Reclaiming mediumship is an act of reclaiming the sacred feminine in all its forms.

For men and masculine-presenting mediums, the witch wound may manifest as a fear of vulnerability, a reluctance to admit sensitivity, or a pressure to perform rather than intuit. They too carry ancestral memories of punishment for deviating from rigid gender norms. The healer, the dreamer, the empath, and the seer have not always had safe spaces in which to exist as men.

Healing the witch wound means creating new narratives for all genders and narratives where sensitivity is strength, where spirit belongs to everyone, and where intuition is a birthright.

Mediumship, at its core, is an act of resistance against systems that would prefer we remain asleep. When a medium channels love, they interrupt cycles of violence. When a medium speaks truth, they dismantle silence. When a medium trusts their knowing, they defy centuries of conditioning. Every session, every circle, every conversation is a spell of remembering. A spell that says, we are not afraid anymore. We are not broken. We are rising.

It is important to remember that the witch wound is not something to get over. It is something to honour. It shaped us, yes. But it does not define us. It was a chapter, not the whole story. The gift of the wound is that it awakens us to the value of what was once suppressed. It teaches us to cherish our gifts rather than hide them. It reminds us that healing is never just for the self. It ripples through bloodlines, timelines, and future generations.

To be a medium today is to be part of this great healing. We are the descendants of those who could not speak. We are the ones who were born to remember. We carry not only the wound but the wisdom.

The medicine. The fire. As we step forward, trembling perhaps, but steady, we offer that medicine to the world. We speak. We see. We serve and in doing so, we heal not only ourselves, but the ancestors, the collective, and the earth itself.

This is the true work of the medium, not only to deliver messages but to be the message. A living reminder that no wound is stronger than love. No silence is greater than the truth. No darkness can extinguish the spirit that refuses to forget who it is.

Reflection Questions: The Witch Wound and the Medium's Inherited Fear

1. Do I carry a deep, sometimes unexplainable fear of being seen, judged, or punished for my spiritual gifts?

2. What memories, dreams, or past life impressions suggest that I may have been silenced, shamed, or harmed for my intuition before?

3. When I speak my truth in a reading, do I feel confident, or do I brace for backlash, disbelief, or abandonment?

4. Have I ever hidden my mediumship or spiritual practices from others out of fear of rejection, ridicule, or danger?

5. How has my ancestral lineage shaped my relationship with intuition, feminine power, and spiritual authority?

6. In what ways do I censor or downplay my gift to appear "safe," "normal," or more acceptable to others?

7. What part of me still believes that being spiritual, intuitive, or different might cost me love, belonging, or safety?

8. If I fully embraced my mediumship without fear of persecution, what would change in the way I serve, speak, and show up in the world?

9. What ancestral women or spiritual lineages do I feel connected to and how might their unhealed pain still live within me or be asking to be voiced through me?

10. What rituals, practices, or affirmations help me reclaim my spiritual power without fear and how can I honour those who came before me by fully standing in my truth?

28. Illness as Initiation – The Wounded Body and the Awakened Soul

Illness is rarely seen as a spiritual teacher. In most societies, it is viewed through a strictly medical lens, something to be treated, managed, or eliminated as quickly as possible. The language of illness is one of war: we fight it, we battle it, we survive it.

This framing, while understandable, often misses the deeper invitation that profound illness can carry. For many mediums and spiritual practitioners, physical illness is not only a crisis but a calling. It is an initiation.

It is the moment when the body speaks what the soul has long tried to whisper. It is when the spirit world begins to stir within the very cells of the flesh. It is the descent that precedes awakening.

Not all illness is spiritual, and not all suffering is sacred. But for the medium, illness often marks a threshold. It interrupts life in a way that forces a revaluation of identity, purpose, and presence. The routines of daily living fall apart. The ego is stripped of control. The future becomes uncertain. In this vulnerability, something ancient is activated. The soul begins to emerge through the cracks.

The medium, who may have spent years developing clairvoyance or energy reading, is now brought to the most intimate and demanding teacher of all; their own body.

The wounded body becomes the temple. It becomes the altar where the medium must sit, breathe, and listen. No longer able to bypass the physical, the medium must bring all of their awareness into the sensations, fears, and fatigue of the moment. This grounding into the body, though painful is what makes the awakening real.

Mediumship is not a floating gift. It is not abstract. It lives in the skin, the breath, the rhythm of the heart. When illness strips everything else away, the medium learns how spirit speaks not only from beyond, but from within.

Illness often opens the door to deeper sensitivity. As the body becomes more attuned to pain, medication, sleep cycles, or nourishment, the soul becomes more attuned to subtle energies.

A medium in recovery may begin to hear new messages, feel new presences, or access deeper levels of emotional truth. The body's fragility becomes a tuning fork. It no longer filters or denies. It reveals. In this rawness, the messages that come through are often more compassionate, more human, more honest. The medium becomes less concerned with performance and more focused on presence. They no longer seek to impress. They seek to serve.

There is a long history of spiritual illness across cultures. In shamanic traditions, the wounded healer is often marked by a serious illness or near-death experience. This crisis is not punishment but preparation.

It is understood that the person being called into spiritual service must undergo a profound transformation, one that reshapes their identity and deepens their empathy. The sickness is the teacher. It rearranges the inner world so that the person can carry the medicine. In these traditions, healing does not always mean curing. It means becoming whole in a new way.

It means becoming a bridge between worlds.

In modern spiritual circles, this understanding is returning.

More and more mediums are speaking openly about their health journeys, the diagnoses, the hospital stays, the medications, the surgeries, the pain. They are rejecting the illusion that a spiritual person must always be radiant, pain-free, or energetically pristine. Instead, they are showing that the path of the medium is often one of brokenness and rebuilding.

They are revealing that vulnerability is not a weakness but a doorway. Through illness, the medium becomes more human. And through that humanity, they become more available to spirit.

Illness also confronts the medium with their mortality. This confrontation is not comfortable, but it is clarifying. It strips away illusions. It reveals what matters and what does not. The medium who has sat on the edge of death gains a perspective that no course or book can offer. They know what it is to fear the unknown. They know what it is to let go of control. And they know what it is to be held by something unseen.

This knowledge changes everything. It deepens the messages. It softens the voice. It makes every word count.

One of the most profound shifts that happens during illness is the collapse of identity. The medium may no longer be able to perform their roles, fulfill their obligations, or meet their own expectations. This loss can feel devastating. But in that collapse, something true is revealed.

The medium is not their work. They are not their readings, their clients, their image. They are a soul in a body, breathing through pain, learning how to love themselves even in stillness. This self-love becomes the foundation of everything. When the medium reemerges, they do so not with ego but with essence. They carry authenticity that cannot be faked.

For those who live with chronic illness, this journey does not end. There is no linear path. There are days of strength and days of surrender. The medium learns how to be in relationship with their body rather than at war with it. They learn how to pace, to rest, to say no. They learn how to ask for help. These are not spiritual failures.

They are spiritual teachings. The body becomes a guide, constantly reminding the medium of what is real and what is needed.

This ongoing conversation between soul and flesh becomes part of the medium's channel. The messages that come through are no longer separate from the medium's experience. They are infused with it. This creates deeper resonance. Clients feel it. Spirit honours it.

There is also a collective layer to this initiation. Illness often isolates. But it also connects. The medium who has suffered becomes a mirror for others who suffer. They become a voice for those who are still silent. They bring compassion not only to the spirit world but to the human world. They become bridge walkers, not only between life and death, but between illness and hope, despair and meaning. Their presence says, I have been there. I am still there. And you are not alone.

Mediums who experience illness may also become more aware of the energetic roots of disease. This does not mean blaming oneself for getting sick. It means listening. Sometimes illness arises from ancestral trauma, unprocessed grief, emotional repression, or spiritual disconnection.

The medium learns how to read the body not just as a biological machine but as an energetic map. They begin to understand how unspoken truths can lodge in the liver, how heartbreak can tighten the lungs, how fear can grip the gut. This awareness allows for multidimensional healing. The medium can work not only with spirit guides but with the organs, the cells, the energetic fields of the body. They become healers in the fullest sense.

But this path also requires discernment. Not all messages about illness are helpful. Some spiritual teachings have caused harm by suggesting that all illness is the result of negative thinking or poor vibration. These ideas are simplistic and shaming. They ignore the complexity of human life, genetics, environment, and injustice.

The medium must be careful not to fall into this trap. Illness is not always a sign of failure. It is not a punishment. It is not evidence of being unspiritual. It is a sacred experience that deserves compassion, nuance, and humility.

The medium who embraces their illness as initiation walks a path of great depth. They do not glamorize suffering, but they do recognize its alchemy. They know that pain can open portals. They know that fatigue can teach surrender. They know that stillness can be filled with spirit. They stop chasing perfection. They stop pretending to be invincible. They become real. And in that realness, spirit finds its clearest voice.

Rest becomes a spiritual practice. Slowness becomes a gift. Presence becomes the medicine. The medium no longer pushes against the body. They listen to it. They honor its rhythms. They let it be a temple, even when it aches. This sacred embodiment is the future of mediumship. It is not about escaping the body to reach spirit. It is about descending into the body so that spirit can be felt fully. It is about making peace with the vessel and allowing it to be holy.

Some mediums will emerge from illness transformed. Others will carry it with them for life. Both paths are valid. Both paths are sacred.

What matters is not whether the body is healed but whether the soul has awakened. What matters is the depth of truth that emerges, the gentleness that grows, the wisdom that is embodied.

Illness strips away illusion. It makes us honest. It brings us home. For the medium, this homecoming is not the end of the journey. It is the beginning of a deeper one. One where every breath is a message. One where every scar is a symbol. One where the body and the spirit walk hand in hand.

Reflection Questions: Illness as Initiation – The Wounded Body and the Awakened Soul

1. How has illness, injury, or chronic pain changed the way I listen to my body and to spirit?

2. Did my spiritual awakening begin or deepen through a health crisis, and what was spirit trying to show me in that experience?

3. What emotional wounds may have manifested physically in my body, asking to be acknowledged and healed?

4. In what ways have I judged or resented my body and how has that shaped my connection to intuition and mediumship?

5. Have I ever experienced moments of spiritual clarity or connection during times of physical vulnerability?

6. What roles have surrender, stillness, and solitude played in the relationship between my healing and my spiritual growth?

7. What beliefs about worthiness, productivity, or strength did I have to release in order to honour my body as a sacred teacher?

8. How does my mediumship feel different when I am in pain, in recovery, or in deep rest?

9. Can I see my illness not as punishment or limitation, but as an invitation into a deeper kind of presence and truth?

10. If I could speak to the part of me that experienced illness as a spiritual initiation, what wisdom would it now offer me and others?

29. Ethical Boundaries and Energetic Responsibility in Mediumship

Mediumship is a sacred art, a profound act of connection between the living and the spirit world. But it is also a responsibility. When a person opens themselves to channel the voices, visions, and impressions of the unseen, they are not only receiving energy, they are also transmitting it.

This transmission does not happen in a vacuum. It flows through the body, through the aura, through intention, and most importantly, through ethical awareness. Ethical boundaries and energetic responsibility are not side notes to the practice of mediumship. They are its foundation. Without them, the work becomes distorted. Without them, the medium becomes vulnerable to burnout, manipulation, or harm.

Ethical boundaries begin with the recognition that mediumship is a form of service. It is not about proving power. It is not about performance. It is not about satisfying curiosity. It is a sacred act of healing and remembrance that requires clarity, humility, and consent.

Every time a medium steps into session, they must ask themselves: Why am I doing this? For whom am I opening? What energy am I welcoming? What do I believe about this work? These questions may seem philosophical, but they are vital. They shape the entire energetic field of the reading. They determine whether the session becomes a space of empowerment or confusion.

One of the first ethical principles in mediumship is consent. Just as in physical life, spirit communication must be entered with permission. It is unethical for a medium to approach someone and begin sharing spirit messages without being invited to do so. This is energetic trespassing.

Even if the medium senses a spirit around someone, it is not their right to speak unless that person opens the door. Mediums must respect boundaries both in the physical world and in the spirit world. They must ask spirit to step back if the space is not appropriate. They must trust that the right messages come in the right timing.

Consent also means recognizing that some people are not ready to hear from the spirit world. They may be grieving, frightened, sceptical, or unsure. The medium must be sensitive to these emotional states. They must never push. They must never try to convince. Their role is to hold space, not to dominate it. This applies especially in group settings, public demonstrations, or spiritual gatherings.

Just because a message is available does not mean it must be delivered. The medium must always consider the impact, not just the information.

Another aspect of ethical mediumship is accuracy and integrity. Mediums are human. They will not always be right. This is normal and natural. What matters is how they hold that reality. Are they willing to admit when something does not land? Do they leave room for uncertainty? Do they allow the client to interpret rather than force validation?

A responsible medium does not need to be perfect. They need to be honest. They need to say, This is what I am sensing. Does this resonate with you? They need to remain in dialogue, not monologue. The client's experience matters as much as the message.

Energetic responsibility also involves managing one's own frequency. Mediumship is not just about opening to spirit, it is about maintaining an energetic field that is clean, stable, and grounded. This means the medium must take care of their emotional, physical, and spiritual well-being.

If they are exhausted, overwhelmed, or emotionally triggered, it is not the time to offer readings. The state of the medium directly influences the quality of the connection. Spirit can only work clearly through a vessel that is cared for. This does not mean being perfect. It means being aware. It means being honest about capacity. It means knowing when to pause.

Clearing energy between sessions is essential. When a medium holds space for grief, trauma, or spiritual emotion, that energy can linger. It can attach to the aura or settle in the body. Without proper clearing, the medium begins to carry other people's pain. Over time, this leads to emotional fatigue, physical symptoms, or spiritual confusion.

Simple practices such as smudging, salt baths, grounding meditations, or breathwork can help release residual energy. More complex clearing may involve calling on guides, using sound healing, or performing intentional rituals. The method is less important than the consistency.

Energetic hygiene is not optional. It is the spiritual equivalent of washing your hands after surgery.

Another layer of ethical awareness involves the type of messages shared. Spirit may sometimes bring through difficult or sensitive information. Death, trauma, addiction, or unresolved conflict may arise.

The medium must handle these topics with the utmost care. They must never use spirit messages to shock, shame, or sensationalize. Even if a message is accurate, the way it is delivered matters. Spirit often chooses symbols or impressions that are subtle and symbolic rather than blunt or harsh.

The medium should follow this example. Speak with gentleness. Deliver truth with kindness. Remember that behind every message is a person with a heart.

Boundaries must also be maintained after the session ends. A reading is a sacred container. It is not a personal relationship. The medium should avoid becoming entangled with clients emotionally, financially, or spiritually. They are not therapists, nor are they saviours.

Their job is to offer insight and connection, not dependency. Clients must be empowered to make their own decisions, process their own healing, and seek additional support when needed. The medium must know when to step back.

When a client becomes overly attached or dependent, it is the medium's ethical duty to redirect them. Sometimes the most loving act is to say, I think our work is complete for now.

Confidentiality is another cornerstone of ethical mediumship. The stories shared in sessions are often deeply personal and emotionally charged. The medium must treat these stories with respect and discretion. Unless given explicit permission, they should not repeat details, even anonymously.

The trust between client and medium is sacred. It is what allows the session to become a space of deep healing. Once that trust is broken, the integrity of the work collapses.

Energetic responsibility also includes how the medium interacts with the spirit world. Not all spirits are meant to be channelled. Not all energies are of the highest vibration. The medium must develop discernment. They must know how to tell the difference between a guide and a trickster, between a true ancestor and a lingering imprint.

This requires ongoing spiritual development, protection practices, and a clear connection to one's own higher self. The medium should never assume that all spirits who come forward are safe or helpful. They must learn to listen deeply, to question gently, and to protect their channel. Just as a therapist would not allow anyone to walk into their office uninvited, the medium must be selective about who they allow into their field.

There is also an ethical responsibility to continue learning. Mediumship is not a fixed skill. It evolves. It deepens. The world changes, and so do the needs of the people we serve. The ethical medium remains curious. They study psychology, trauma, cultural awareness, and spiritual diversity. They listen to teachers, guides, and peers. They examine their own biases. They seek feedback. They know that to serve spirit is to stay humble. There is always more to understand.

Cultural sensitivity is a growing area of ethical responsibility. Mediums must be aware of the traditions, beliefs, and wounds that shape their clients' experiences. They must avoid appropriating practices from cultures that are not theirs without permission or proper understanding. They must be mindful of the language they use.

Spirit does not belong to one religion or one race. The medium must create inclusive space, one where all people feel seen, safe, and respected.

Pricing and accessibility also fall under ethical consideration. Mediums deserve to be paid. Their time, energy, and training have value. However, they must also be honest about what they offer. They should not exaggerate their abilities or make promises they cannot keep. They should not create fear in order to sell a service. Ethical pricing reflects the energy exchanged, not the desperation of the client. Some mediums choose to offer sliding scales, scholarships, or free community events as a way to balance income with service. Each medium must decide what aligns with their values.

Ultimately, ethical mediumship is about intention. It is about coming to work with a clean heart. It is about remembering that this path is not about ego, fame, or control.

It is about healing. It is about truth. It is about the sacred act of being a channel for love, remembrance, and guidance.

Every time a medium opens the door to spirit, they step into a lineage of service that stretches beyond time. They are the bridge. They are the witness. They are the voice.

To walk this path with integrity is to honour the trust placed in us by the living and the dead. It is to carry the weight of our influence with care. It is to know that we do not just speak for spirit. We embody it. In our choices. In our boundaries. In our presence. That is the truest message of all.

Reflection Questions: Ethical Boundaries and Energetic Responsibility in Mediumship

1. Do I understand the difference between being of service and being responsible for someone's healing or outcome?

2. Have I ever delivered a message that I intuitively knew should have been held back or softened and what did I learn from that experience?

3. What are my personal ethical boundaries when it comes to sharing difficult, shocking, or private information from spirit?

4. Do I have clear energetic boundaries in place before, during, and after readings, or do I absorb and carry others' energy unconsciously?

5. How do I protect the emotional safety of the sitter, especially when spirit brings through sensitive or unresolved information?

6. When I feel ego or performance energy rising during a reading, how do I pause, reset, or return to authentic connection?

7. Do I regularly reflect on the quality and impact of my work, or have I become desensitised to the responsibility of my role?

8. Am I willing to say no, stop a reading, or redirect a session if I feel it is no longer in alignment with truth or safety?

9. What do I do to ethically discharge or cleanse the energy I've carried after being in sacred space with someone else's grief or story?

10. If spirit held a mirror to my mediumship today, would it reflect responsibility, integrity, and compassion or is there somewhere I am being invited to grow?

30. The Psychology of the Spiritually Gifted Child

In every generation, there are children who see beyond the veil. They are born with senses attuned not only to the physical world but also to realms that others have forgotten. They speak of ancestors they have never met. They describe dreams with layers of meaning far beyond their years. They speak with an awareness of death that is not fearful, but familiar.

These are the spiritually gifted children. Their presence is not new. They have always walked among us. But in this time of awakening, they are being recognized, and their gifts are finally being understood through the dual lens of psychology and spirituality.

To understand the spiritually gifted child is to remember that mediumship does not suddenly appear in adulthood. It begins as a whisper in early life. It may begin with invisible friends, prophetic dreams, or unexplained knowledge. These children often speak about things they have not been taught. They may talk about heaven as if they remember it. They may see auras, sense illness in others, or report communication from those who have passed away.

In most families, this awareness is not met with encouragement. It is often dismissed, pathologized, or feared. This is not out of malice. It is because the world is not yet fully comfortable with what these children represent.

From a psychological standpoint, the gifted child experiences the world with heightened sensitivity. Their nervous systems are more reactive. They feel deeply, think profoundly, and observe everything. They may cry easily, not because they are fragile, but because they are attuned to emotional undercurrents that others overlook. They may become overwhelmed in crowds, loud environments, or chaotic family systems. Their tantrums may not stem from defiance but from overstimulation. Their silence may not mean withdrawal but inner processing of a reality that is multilayered and intense.

Spiritually gifted children often feel different. Even before they can name it, they sense that they are not like the others. This can create loneliness. They may struggle to find peers who understand them. They may internalize their uniqueness as wrongness. They may learn to hide their gifts to avoid ridicule. In time, they may even begin to question their own experiences. Did I really see that spirit? Did I imagine that voice?

This self-doubt becomes the beginning of spiritual amnesia.

The child begins to close the door, not because they want to, but because the world has told them it is not safe to leave it open.

There is also a deep connection between spiritually gifted children and trauma. Not all gifted children are traumatized, but many have experienced early emotional ruptures. Sometimes it is a loss, a near-death experience, a chronically ill parent, or a home filled with unspoken emotion.

These experiences open the child to the unseen. In trauma, the boundary between worlds thins.

The child who has been hurt may leave their body, seeking safety in the spiritual world. What begins as survival can evolve into sacred sight. They begin to see what others do not. But without guidance, this becomes a burden. They may feel haunted, frightened, or overwhelmed by energies they do not know how to manage.

The psychology of the spiritually gifted child must account for both their emotional development and their spiritual reality. They need validation that their experiences are real, even if others cannot see them. They need language for what they feel. They need to be told, not that they are strange, but that they are gifted. They need tools to protect their energy, to regulate their emotions, and to discern between imagination and intuition. These are not indulgences. They are necessities for healthy development.

Parental support is vital. When a parent honours their child's spiritual awareness, the child blossoms. They feel safe to speak. They feel safe to ask questions. They do not feel the need to hide. But when a parent is afraid, dismissive, or rigidly sceptical, the child internalizes the message that their truth is dangerous. They may shut down their gifts, or worse, begin to believe that something is wrong with them.

Many adult mediums trace their wounds back to childhood moments when their insight was met with laughter or punishment. Healing begins with being seen.

Education systems are not always equipped to recognize spiritual giftedness. Children who are clairaudient may be misdiagnosed with auditory hallucinations. Children who see spirits may be labelled as having delusions. Children who become overwhelmed by emotion may be classified as oppositional, anxious, or defiant.

These labels, while sometimes helpful in creating access to support, can also become limiting. They reduce a multidimensional experience to a clinical symptom. Spiritually gifted children require a different lens, one that is holistic, compassionate, and curious. They need educators, therapists, and mentors who understand that sensitivity is not a flaw. It is a gift in need of care.

For mediums who were once these children, remembering is both healing and painful. It may bring tears to recall the times you saw things you could not explain, the times you knew things no one believed, the times you cried, and no one understood why. But it is also a doorway to reclaiming the earliest roots of your gift.

To become the medium you are today, you must acknowledge the child who saw spirit first. You must thank them. You must hold them. You must listen to what they still remember.

There is an emotional intensity in spiritually gifted children that must be handled with reverence. These children do not just feel their own feelings, they absorb the emotions of those around them. They may cry in response to someone else's sadness. They may feel agitated in places where trauma lingers. They may carry the moods of a household without knowing why. This makes energetic boundaries essential.

Teaching children how to discern what is theirs and what is not is one of the most powerful forms of protection. Breathwork, visualization, grounding practices, and aura cleansing can all be taught in age-appropriate ways. When a child knows how to clear their field, they feel safer in their own skin.

Dreams are another key aspect of a gifted child's world. Many children receive messages in their sleep. They may have recurring dreams of past lives, messages from deceased loved ones, or symbolic visions of events to come.

Dreams are often the safest space for spirit to make contact. They bypass the intellect. They offer pure imagery. Helping children understand their dreams is a way of honouring their inner world. Encouraging dream journaling, drawing, or storytelling gives form to their experiences. It shows them that their inner life matters.

Some children also speak of memories that do not belong to this life. They may describe details of historical periods, geographic locations, or cultural practices they have never encountered. They may have unexplained fears or fascinations that link to past life trauma. This can be deeply confusing if not acknowledged.

A child who is terrified of drowning for no reason may be reliving a death memory. A child who insists they used to live in a different country may be remembering a soul imprint. Whether or not a parent or teacher believes in reincarnation, the child's emotional experience is real and deserves validation. Asking gentle questions, allowing expression, and remaining open can provide the safety needed for healing to begin.

Spiritually gifted children may also be natural mediums. They may spontaneously speak messages from spirit. They may sense when someone is near death. They may feel the presence of a departed loved one before anyone else knows they are gone. This can be beautiful, but it can also be terrifying.

Children need to be taught that they have choice. They can ask spirit to come back later. They can set boundaries. They can say no. Just as we teach children not to talk to strangers, we must teach them how to interact with spirit safely. Spiritual autonomy is as important as physical safety.

As these children grow, their gifts may evolve. Some will become professional mediums. Others will become artists, teachers, caregivers, or leaders. Not all spiritually gifted children grow up to work with spirit directly.

But the awareness remains. It shapes their compassion, their intuition, their wisdom. They carry the medicine of connection into whatever path they choose. The world needs these souls. It needs their truth, their vision, their depth.

For those who guide these children, whether as parents, mentors, or spiritual teachers, the role is sacred. It is not about control. It is about protection and empowerment. It is about walking alongside them, not above them.

It is about helping them understand the difference between fear and intuition, between fantasy and vision, between ego and soul. These children are not here to be molded into the expectations of others. They are here to remember who they are.

There will be challenges. There will be resistance. There may be times when the child rejects their gift. There may be times when they struggle with anxiety, depression, or spiritual disconnection. These are not failures. They are part of the journey.

The veil between worlds is thin, but so is the veil between spiritual awakening and emotional overwhelm. The child must be held with both spiritual insight and psychological skill. Therapy, energy work, spiritual education, and community support must all work together. No single approach is enough. The child is a multidimensional being. Their care must reflect that truth.

Mediumship begins in childhood. Not always in practice, but in sensitivity. The seeds are planted early. They are watered by experience. They are shaped by love and fear alike. When we honour the psychology of the spiritually gifted child, we do more than protect them; we protect the future of spiritual connection itself.

We create a world where intuition is not shamed, where the invisible is not denied, and where the voices of spirit are heard clearly because the vessels carrying them have been seen, supported, and set free.

The mediumship child within is the part of you who first sensed the unseen, who felt the presence of spirit before knowing what it meant, who loved deeply, empathized instinctively, and was often overwhelmed by emotions that didn't seem to belong to them. This inner child is sacred.

They are the origin of your gift, the spark that allowed you to hear whispers, see shadows, or feel things others dismissed. Protecting them means acknowledging that your sensitivity didn't begin as a skill, it began as vulnerability.

To honour this part of yourself is to stop forcing, proving, or overextending. It means gently reminding that younger version of you: *"You are safe now. You no longer have to carry this alone."*

Protection for the mediumship child comes through loving boundaries, rest, and the conscious choice to create safety in your spiritual practice. When you protect this inner part of yourself, you stop using your gift as a way to seek validation and instead begin to use it as an expression of truth.

Speak kindly to that inner child. Let them know that the energy you channel will be filtered through wisdom, not sacrifice. That you will listen to your needs first, before anyone else's demands. For when the mediumship child feels safe, the channel becomes clearer. The gift becomes lighter. And your relationship with spirit becomes not a burden to survive, but a miracle to share.

Reflection Questions: The Psychology of the Spiritually Gifted Child

1. When did I first feel different, sensitive, or aware of things others could not see or feel?

2. How did my caregivers or environment respond to my early spiritual or intuitive experiences; were they nurtured, dismissed, or feared?

3. Did I learn to suppress my sensitivity to fit in, stay safe, or avoid being misunderstood?

4. What emotions did I most often feel as a child; were they mine, or was I absorbing the energy of others?

5. Was I ever punished or shamed for being "too emotional," "too intense," or "too imaginative"?

6. How did I cope with feeling unseen, energetically overwhelmed, or emotionally responsible for others as a child?

7. Do I still carry childhood beliefs that my intuition is dangerous, shameful, or untrustworthy?

8. What spiritual memories, dreams, or inner knowing from childhood have stayed with me—and what might they be trying to teach me now?

9. Did I experience fear of the dark, death, or the unknown as a child and how were those fears connected to my spiritual gifts?

10. When I reflect on my inner child now, what does they still long for in terms of safety, validation, and expression?

11. What part of my childhood intuition do I now consider sacred and how do I reconnect with it today?

12. How has my early experience of being spiritually gifted shaped my adult relationships, boundaries, and identity?

13. What unmet emotional needs from childhood still echo in my mediumship today?

14. How can I become the protector and guide my younger self needed, both for myself and the people I serve through spirit?

15. If I could speak to the spiritually gifted child I once was, what words of comfort, empowerment, or truth would I give them now?

31. Navigating Dark Energies and Psychic Interference

There is a truth that every experienced medium eventually learns. Not all energies encountered in the unseen realms are light. While mediumship is a sacred bridge that often delivers comfort, healing, and divine insight, it also traverses territories of shadow.

Just as the physical world contains both beauty and pain, the spiritual world holds a spectrum of energies. Some are confused, bound, or disruptive. Others are deceptive, manipulative, or parasitic.

Navigating dark energies and psychic interference is not about cultivating fear. It is about developing discernment. It is about learning to see clearly without becoming lost in what is seen. And it is about understanding that true power does not lie in dominance, but in alignment.

Every medium, at some point in their development, will encounter darker or more chaotic energies. These experiences are not signs of failure. They are not punishments. They are invitations to deepen, to clarify, and to ground.

There are many reasons why a dark energy might appear. Sometimes it is a fragment of unresolved trauma. Sometimes it is a lingering spirit who has not yet crossed over. Sometimes it is an energetic parasite feeding off emotional instability. Other times, it is not external at all, but a projection of the medium's own shadow, the parts of the psyche that have not yet been integrated or healed.

Discernment is the first skill a medium must develop when facing these energies. Not everything that presents as frightening is dangerous. A confused or earthbound spirit may feel heavy or chaotic, but this does not mean it intends harm.

In fact, many lost souls are simply seeking help. They are reaching out in the only way they know. The medium must be able to assess the frequency of the energy without rushing to judgment. Is it malicious or simply unsettled? Is it a presence that wants to communicate or a residue of past suffering? Is it attached to a person or place?

These questions must be asked not from fear, but from curiosity and clarity.

Fear is the greatest amplifier of darkness. When a medium becomes afraid, their vibration lowers. This creates a vulnerability. The key is to remain in sovereignty.

Sovereignty means knowing who you are. It means grounding into your own power, your own boundaries, your own light.

Darkness can only enter where there is permission or resonance. If the medium holds unresolved fear, unprocessed trauma, or unexamined beliefs, these can become doorways. This is not a judgment. It is an opportunity. Every encounter with shadow is a mirror. It shows the medium where their field is porous, where their energy is leaking, where healing is needed.

Protection is essential. Not because the medium is constantly under threat, but because they are constantly open. Protection is not about building walls.

Mediumship protection is about setting clear energetic filters. These filters are created through intention, practice, and alignment.

Daily rituals can include grounding into the earth, calling in protective guides, visualizing a shield of light, and cleansing the aura after sessions. Herbs like sage, mugwort, or rosemary can support. Crystals like black tourmaline, obsidian, or smoky quartz can help anchor the field. But protection is not just about tools. It is about vibration. A clear, loving, and confident vibration naturally repels lower energies.

When a medium is in integrity with themselves, they are not easy to access.

Sometimes psychic interference comes not from spirit, but from living people. This may sound strange, but thoughts and emotions are energy. When someone projects jealousy, anger, or obsession toward a medium, that energy can be felt. In some cases, it may create interference in readings, dreams, or even the medium's physical body. This is why energetic hygiene must extend beyond sessions.

The medium must learn how to cut cords, return energy to sender, and create space from people whose presence drains or disturbs their field. Not all connections are meant to be maintained. Loving detachment is a form of spiritual safety.

There are also entities that are not human and have never been. These energies can be more complex. Some are neutral. Others are mischievous. A few are genuinely malevolent. These are rare but real.

The medium must never become obsessed with them, but they must be aware. If an energy presents itself as a spirit guide but begins to cause fear, dependency, or confusion, it is not a guide. True guides empower. They uplift. They bring clarity and peace. Trickster energies often play on the ego. They may flatter the medium, promise power, or flood them with chaotic visions. These energies thrive on attention. The antidote is silence, clarity, and dismissal.

The medium must assert, You are not welcome here. Return to the light. The most powerful tools are command and compassion.

Mediums must also understand psychic attack. This term is often misunderstood and sensationalized, but it simply refers to energetic intrusion. It can be intentional or unintentional. A former partner thinking obsessively about the medium. A jealous peer sending negative thoughts. A client projecting fear after a difficult session. These are forms of psychic entanglement. They do not always come from malice. But they require attention.

The medium must clear their field regularly. They must reclaim their energy daily. They must avoid the illusion that love means constant openness. Boundaries are not barriers to spirit. They are the framework that makes spirit work safe and sustainable.

Dark energy is also sometimes the product of collective pain. Mediums who are highly empathic may begin to channel the suffering of the world.

They may feel waves of despair, grief, or anxiety that are not theirs. These are not attachments. They are energetic downloads.

The medium becomes a vessel not just for individual messages but for the voice of the collective unconscious. This is powerful work, but it is not easy. The medium must ground deeply. They must transmute, not absorb. They must become the flame, not the ash. This requires discipline, rest, and community. No medium can do this alone.

The danger in working with dark energy is not the darkness itself, it is the medium's attachment to it. Some mediums become fascinated. They begin to chase the strange, the shocking, the terrifying. They feel more powerful when facing demons or clearing curses. But this is a trap. True power does not need drama. True service does not need spectacle.

The medium who becomes addicted to shadow work risks losing the light. They may begin to believe that everything is an attack, that everyone is cursed, that every spirit is malevolent. This is not discernment. This is imbalance. The work must always return to love.

Love is the ultimate clearing force. Not romantic love, but divine love. The love that says, I see you, even in your confusion. I forgive you, even in your pain. I release you, because you do not belong here. This love does not deny the existence of darkness. It transforms it. A medium working in love becomes untouchable. Not because they are perfect, but because they are aligned. They are serving truth.

Sometimes dark energy appears not as an external force but as an inner voice. The critic. The doubter. The saboteur. This is psychic interference of a different kind. It is the residue of old programming, ancestral fear, or past life trauma. It tells the medium they are not good enough. It whispers that they are making it all up. It warns them to stop before they are exposed. This is the voice of the witch wound, the trauma memory, the inner child. It is not to be banished but healed.

The medium must sit with this voice. They must say, I hear you. I know why you are scared. But we are safe now. We are ready. You do not have to protect me anymore.

Mediumship is a sacred responsibility. It is not for the faint of heart. It is not for those seeking fame, power, or spiritual shortcuts. It is for those willing to stand in the storm and still speak of love. It is for those who will not flinch when the shadows rise, but who will light the candle anyway.

To navigate dark energies is not to seek them out. It is to know how to walk through them when they appear. It is to know when to act, when to release, when to call for help. It is to trust your guides. It is to trust your training. It is to trust your soul.

In the end, all energy seeks return. The lost seek direction. The angry seek healing. The bound seek release. The medium is the one who offers that bridge, not by force, but by light. When we understand this, darkness loses its power.

It becomes a teacher. A shadow that points to the flame. The medium walks on, grounded, clear, protected, and devoted to the work.

To walk as a medium is to walk between worlds, and often, between light and shadow. There are moments when your work will draw you into the deeper spaces of human suffering grief, trauma, fear, and loss. In those moments, it is essential to understand that your light is not a weapon to fight the darkness, but a sacred frequency to be held with care.

Protecting your mediumship light means remembering that you are not here to absorb pain, but to witness and transmit healing through grounded presence. You are not the solution; you are the bridge and that bridge must be strong, stable, and clear, or it will crumble under the weight of energy not meant to be yours.

Shadow work is a necessary part of true mediumship, because spirit will not only bring love and peace, but also truths that are heavy, unresolved, or buried. In facing these shadows, mediums often feel the temptation to dim their light, to take on the suffering of others, or to lose themselves in the stories of the departed. Protecting your light requires spiritual discipline.

It means returning daily to your own source of nourishment, prayer, ritual, silence, nature, or rest. It means grounding after every session, clearing your field, and reaffirming your intention: *"I serve from fullness, not from depletion. I walk with light, but I do not carry what is not mine."*

It is also vital to surround your mediumship practice with energetic and emotional boundaries. Just as you wouldn't leave your physical door open to anyone at any hour, your spiritual channel must be kept sacred. Protection isn't fear; t's clarity. It's saying no to energies, clients, or spirits that feel chaotic or manipulative. It's trusting that your light is not diminished by saying no but strengthened.

The more protected your light is, the brighter and more sustainable your service becomes and in doing so, you teach others, both in the physical and spiritual realms, how to engage with you from a place of mutual respect and reverence.

Ultimately, protecting your light is an act of love and not just for yourself, but for the work itself. When you are clear, whole, and sovereign, your mediumship becomes more than just communication with spirit, it becomes a living medicine.

You show others that it is possible to stand in shadow without losing your radiance. You remind the grieving, the haunted, and the lost that there is a way through. And most importantly, you show yourself that your light was never meant to be sacrificed. It was meant to guide, to illuminate, and to endure.

That is the sacred path of the medium who chooses to serve with soul.

Reflection Questions: Navigating Dark Energies and Psychic Interference

1. How do I personally define "dark energy" or psychic interference and what does it bring up in me emotionally?

2. Have I ever encountered a spiritual presence or energetic experience that felt draining, deceptive, or unsafe?

3. When I feel fear during a reading or spiritual experience, how do I respond, do I freeze, flee, fight, or spiritually bypass?

4. What are the signs; emotional, physical, or intuitive, that I am in the presence of unbalanced or disruptive energy?

5. Do I trust myself to discern between a genuine spirit message and an energetic manipulation or interference?

6. Have I ever doubted my gift after encountering something heavy or dark and how did I find my way back to trust?

7. What rituals, practices, or boundaries help me remain grounded and sovereign in the presence of strong or chaotic energies?

8. Do I feel guilt or fear about saying no to certain spirits, energies, or even clients and how does that affect my energetic safety?

9. What is my relationship to spiritual protection and is it rooted in fear, strength, or clarity?

10. Have I unintentionally opened spiritual doors without proper preparation or boundaries and what did I learn from that experience?

11. How do I maintain my energetic hygiene after sessions that leave me feeling disoriented, low, or psychically open?

12. What inner shadows or unconscious fears might make me more vulnerable to spiritual confusion or attachment?

13. Do I have a spiritual support system, guides, mentors, practices, that I can call on when navigating darker spaces?

14. How do I hold space for others who are experiencing psychic interference without becoming entangled in their energy?

15. If I fully trusted my light, my discernment, and my spiritual team, how would I move differently through fear, shadow, and the unknown?

32. The Intersection of Psychology and Trance States

Trance is a word that evokes mystery. It conjures images of deep stillness, altered perception, and communion with something beyond the self.

For mediums, trance is more than a technique. It is a doorway. It is the inner descent into silence where spirit begins to speak. But what is often overlooked is how deeply trance is connected to psychology. The altered states that mediums enter are not merely spiritual experiences.

They are psychological processes that mirror some of the most profound functions of the mind. To understand trance in mediumship is to also understand dissociation, memory, imagination, belief, and emotion. The bridge between psychology and trance is not a narrow crossing. It is a wide landscape filled with insight.

In its simplest form, a trance is a shift in consciousness. The brain moves from its usual waking state into one that is more inwardly focused, more receptive, and more suggestible. The body relaxes. The breath slows. Time becomes elastic. This is not a foreign or rare experience. We enter mild trances every day. Daydreaming, becoming absorbed in music, losing track of time while driving, or feeling detached during intense emotional moments are all examples of natural trance states.

These moments teach us that trance is not about leaving the body. It is about expanding perception. The medium learns to harness this natural ability, deepening it with intention, practice, and spiritual focus.

From a psychological perspective, trance involves the quieting of the analytical mind. This allows access to deeper parts of the psyche, memory, intuition, and even the unconscious. The ego steps back. The inner critic softens.

The medium becomes more attuned to imagery, emotion, and subtle sensation. This state can feel like drifting between waking and sleep. It can feel like falling inward. In this openness, spirit can enter. Not as an external force taking control, but as a resonance. A merging. A joining of energies that feels both personal and beyond.

One of the most important psychological parallels to trance is the concept of dissociation. In trauma studies, dissociation is often described as a coping mechanism. When a person experiences overwhelming emotion or danger, the mind may disconnect from the body or from ordinary awareness.

This can lead to feelings of unreality, emotional numbness, or memory gaps. While this form of dissociation is protective, it can also become a barrier to healing if not integrated. In trance mediumship, however, we see a different kind of dissociation, one that is intentional, temporary, and healing. The medium chooses to step aside. They soften their grip on identity. They allow another presence to move through.

But they do not become lost. They do not abandon themselves. Instead, they return with insight. The trance becomes a sacred dance between surrender and return.

This is why psychological safety is essential in trance work. If a medium carries unhealed trauma, the trance state may inadvertently trigger emotional memories or unresolved pain.

The boundary between spiritual guidance and psychological projection becomes blurred. What feels like a message from spirit may actually be an unmet part of the self-crying out for attention. This does not invalidate the experience. But it does require discernment. The trained medium must know their inner landscape. They must be able to tell the difference between a guide and an inner child, between a soul imprint and a trauma echo. This is not always easy.

It requires self-awareness, reflection, and sometimes therapeutic support. Mediumship does not exist outside of mental health. The two must walk together.

Imagination also plays a critical role in trance. Many people are taught to see imagination as the opposite of truth.

But in mediumship, imagination is the bridge. It is the canvas on which spirit paints. When a medium enters trance, they may receive impressions as images, sounds, symbols, or sensations. These arrive through the imagination. Not as fantasies, but as translations. Spirit communicates in energy. The mind converts that energy into something the medium can perceive. This means that every trance is a co-creation.

The medium's consciousness shapes the message. This does not mean the message is untrue. It means that truth is filtered through the human soul. The medium's vocabulary, life experience, beliefs, and emotional state all play a role. Understanding this helps the medium stay humble and clear. They are not passive channels. They are active participants in the mystery.

The psychology of belief also intersects with trance. What the medium believes about spirit, about themselves, and about the world shapes the trance experience. If they believe that trance is dangerous, they will struggle to relax into it. If they believe they are unworthy, they may block the flow. If they believe that spirit only speaks in certain ways, they may overlook subtle impressions.

Belief is not just mental. It is energetic. It creates pathways or barriers. This is why part of trance training involves identifying and shifting limiting beliefs. The medium must learn to trust their connection, trust their body, and trust their ability to return safely. Without this trust, trance becomes brittle or distorted.

Emotion is another powerful component. Trance is not just mental relaxation. It is emotional surrender. The medium must be willing to feel deeply.

Spirit often communicates through emotional resonance. A sudden wave of sorrow, a burst of joy, a rush of peace, these are messages. They are not always attached to words. They are energetic signatures.

The medium must learn to hold emotion without analysis. To let it pass through. To witness it as a vessel.

This emotional openness is a gift, but it can also be overwhelming. Without emotional regulation, the trance may become chaotic. The medium may cry, shake, or feel drained.

Grounding after trance is not optional. It is sacred integration. The body must be brought back online. The heart must be held gently. The spirit must be thanked.

From a neurological perspective, trance involves shifts in brainwave activity. Waking consciousness is dominated by beta waves, fast, focused, and logical.

As the medium enters trance, their brain slows into alpha and then into theta waves. Theta is the realm of deep meditation, creativity, and subconscious access. It is also the realm where many spiritual phenomena occur.

The medium may receive visions, hear voices, or channel messages in this state. Theta is a fertile ground, but it is also porous. Boundaries must be strong. The medium must anchor themselves before entering and call themselves back clearly when finished.

Without this, the edges of reality can become blurred. The medium may feel disoriented or emotionally raw. Rituals of return are not superstitions. They are psychological reintegration.

Trance also brings up questions of identity. Who am I when I step aside? Who speaks through me? How do I make sense of what I have said or seen? These are profound psychological inquiries. The trance medium must navigate their sense of self with care. They must avoid over-identifying with their channelled persona.

Some mediums give names to the guides they channel. Others speak in different tones or with altered expressions. This can be powerful, but it must be held lightly. The medium must remember their human self. They must return to their body. They must eat, rest, laugh, and live. Trance is a gift, but it is not the whole truth. It is a lens. A window. A glimpse.

In therapeutic settings, trance states are often used for healing. Hypnotherapy, guided imagery, and somatic experiencing all draw on the same principles. They invite the person to enter a softened state, bypass the critical mind, and connect with deeper truths. Mediums who understand this connection can integrate psychological insights into their trance work. They can guide clients not only to receive messages but to experience healing. A spirit may speak of forgiveness.

The medium can then help the client feel that forgiveness in their body. A loved one may come through with a message of reassurance. The medium can help the client breathe into that peace. Trance becomes not just a communication tool, but a container for transformation.

Some mediums fear trance because they associate it with possession. They worry about losing control. But trance is not about being taken over.

It is about choosing to listen more deeply. It is about creating a safe, sacred space within the self. Possession is forceful and uninvited. Trance is consensual and intentional.

The medium invites the guide or spirit. They remain aware. They remain in command. Even if they step far aside, their soul is still sovereign. They can end the connection at any time. This understanding empowers the medium to explore trance without fear. They are not opening themselves to anything.

They are opening to something specific. Something aligned. Something sacred.

As the world continues to awaken spiritually, trance mediumship is becoming more valued. But with that visibility comes responsibility.

The medium must educate their clients about what trance is and what it is not. They must set boundaries around when they will enter trance, how they will return, and what kind of messages they will allow through. They must avoid theatrics. They must resist the urge to impress.

Trance is not a performance. It is a prayer. It is a quieting of the ego so that truth may emerge.

Trance is not reserved for advanced mediums. It is a natural progression of deepening presence. It is accessible to all who are willing to listen deeply. It begins with silence. It continues with trust. It deepens with devotion. There are many forms of trance—from light meditative states to deep full-body channelling.

Each medium finds their own rhythm. There is no hierarchy. What matters is authenticity. What matters is alignment. What matters is love.

In the end, trance is a return to the soul. It is a meeting place between the seen and unseen. It is the space where psychology and spirit hold hands. The brain quiets. The heart opens. The message arrives and the medium, ever humble, ever human, speaks the words that come not from thought, but from truth.

Honouring your gift through the psychology of acceptance means embracing your mediumship not as something to hide, prove, or justify, but as an intrinsic part of who you are.

Acceptance is the moment you stop questioning whether you're "enough" and begin to trust that your gift is valid, even if it doesn't look like anyone else's.

Through this psychological lens, you no longer treat your sensitivity as a flaw but as a finely tuned instrument shaped by your life experiences, emotions, and soul journey. Acceptance integrates the gift into your identity with grace, allowing you to serve from wholeness instead of performance. It shifts the inner dialogue from resistance to reverence, creating space for growth, confidence, and authentic expression.

33. Dissociation Versus Trance – Understanding the Difference

In the landscape of mediumship and altered states of consciousness, there is often confusion between the experiences of trance and dissociation. Both involve shifts in awareness. Both may produce sensations of detachment from ordinary reality.

Both may occur with closed eyes, slowed breath, and altered perception. But despite their surface similarities, dissociation and trance arise from very different roots and lead to very different outcomes.

For mediums and those exploring psychic development, the ability to discern between these two states is essential. It not only ensures safety and clarity, but it also supports the long-term mental, emotional, and spiritual well-being of the practitioner.

Understanding the difference between trance and dissociation is not only a clinical or academic concern, but also a spiritual responsibility.

Trance is an intentional descent. It is a conscious invitation into a state of deeper presence. The medium chooses to relax their mind, slow their breath, and allow their awareness to shift from the external world to the internal landscape. In trance, there is a sense of spaciousness, not numbness.

There is a feeling of openness, not disconnection. The medium remains present, though they may become less focused on the sensory environment. They are not abandoning themselves. Rather, they are softening the noise of the personality so that another voice may emerge. Trance is anchored in consent.

The medium prepares for it, invites it, and closes it with intention. It is a practice of devotion, alignment, and clear spiritual boundaries.

Dissociation, by contrast, is a protective response. It occurs when the mind or body feels overwhelmed, threatened, or emotionally unsafe. In dissociation, a person may suddenly feel distant from their own body or emotions. They may feel as if they are watching themselves from afar, as if life is happening to someone else. This is not an act of spiritual surrender. It is a survival strategy.

The nervous system shifts into a freeze state. The psyche detaches in order to cope.

For many trauma survivors, dissociation becomes a well-worn path. It is not chosen consciously. It arises from a deep need for safety when safety is absent. It is not a spiritual gateway. It is a wound crying for protection and healing.

The danger arises when dissociation is mistaken for trance. A medium may enter a reading or meditation and find themselves spacing out, losing time, or feeling emotionally disconnected. They may interpret this as a sign of deep spiritual contact.

But if the state is rooted in fear, avoidance, or unresolved trauma, the messages they receive may be distorted or incomplete.

Worse, the medium may retraumatize themselves by believing they are spiritually evolving while actually repeating old survival patterns. This is why shadow work is so important in mediumship. The clearer the medium is about their psychological landscape, the safer their spiritual journeys will become. Awareness is the key.

One of the main differences between trance and dissociation is the quality of presence. In trance, the medium remains tethered. Even if they are deeply inward, there is a thread of awareness that can always lead them back. They can speak if needed. They can return to the room. They may be in an altered state, but they are still responsive.

In dissociation, there is often a sense of being absent or unreachable. The person may seem vacant or foggy. They may have trouble recalling what happened during the episode. Their voice may become flat. Their body may feel heavy or numb. They may return from the state feeling confused, anxious, or ungrounded.

Trance tends to leave a sense of peace or clarity. Dissociation often leaves fragmentation.

Another key distinction is the role of emotional regulation. In trance, the medium may feel a surge of emotion, but they remain connected to it. They can move through it. They can integrate it. In dissociation, emotion is often blunted or entirely absent. This is not because the person is truly calm and it is because their system has gone offline.

The body is still carrying the emotion, but the mind has cut the cord. This is why dissociation can be dangerous over time. The unprocessed feelings remain stored in the nervous system. They may manifest later as anxiety, depression, or physical symptoms. Trance, when done with care, helps release emotion. It helps move energy. It helps integrate the spiritual with the emotional.

In terms of brain function, trance and dissociation also differ. Trance states, especially those used in mediumship and deep meditation, typically involve shifts into theta and alpha brainwaves. These states are associated with relaxation, creativity, and spiritual insight. The brain remains active, but in a more receptive and intuitive mode.

Dissociation, particularly in trauma responses, often involves disintegration between different parts of the brain. The prefrontal cortex may go offline. The amygdala may fire rapidly. The body may be in a freeze state while the mind feels blank or detached. These patterns are not conducive to healthy spirit work. They create vulnerability rather than receptivity. They open the door to confusion rather than clarity.

The motivations behind each state are also different. Trance is motivated by trust. The medium trusts themselves. They trust spirit. They trust the process. Dissociation is motivated by fear. The individual may not even know what they are afraid of, but the body remembers. Something in the environment, or even in the inner world, feels unsafe. The dissociative response is not a flaw.

It is an ancient form of protection. But it cannot replace grounded spiritual practice.

A medium who consistently dissociates may receive fragmented messages, lose touch with their physical health, or begin to feel haunted by energies they cannot understand. Grounding is not optional in this work. It is the foundation of everything.

Healing dissociation involves working with the body. The breath. The heart. The inner child. It involves therapy, embodiment practices, and self-compassion. It involves learning that it is safe to feel. Safe to remember. Safe to stay.

For many mediums, healing their dissociative tendencies leads to deeper, clearer, and more joyful connections with spirit. They stop running. They start listening. They discover that the most powerful messages come not from escaping the body, but from inhabiting it fully.

Spirit meets us where we are. Not where we think we should be. When the body and soul are united, the channel is pure.

There is also a spiritual aspect to dissociation that deserves mention. Some souls who have experienced lifetimes of persecution, trauma, or loss may carry energetic imprints of separation. They may find it hard to stay fully present in the body. They may feel more comfortable in the astral or etheric realms. These tendencies are not personal failings.

They are soul memories. But they must be brought into awareness. Mediumship is not about living halfway in spirit and halfway in the world. It is about building a bridge between the two. The medium must be anchored in the human while reaching into the divine. That is what makes them a trustworthy messenger.

Trance work, when practiced with integrity, can actually help heal dissociation. It teaches the medium to relax without fleeing. To open without fragmenting. To listen without losing themselves. But this only works when the trance is entered from a place of safety.

The space must be prepared. The body must be supported. The intention must be clear. Spirit does not rush. The medium must learn to slow down. To notice. To honour their own needs as much as they honour the needs of those they serve. This is not selfishness. It is energetic integrity.

In practical terms, mediums can begin to distinguish between trance and dissociation by tracking their bodily sensations. Are you grounded? Can you feel your feet? Can you sense your breath? Are you emotionally present? Can you describe what you are experiencing? Do you return from the state with clarity and calm, or with confusion and fatigue? Do you feel empowered, or do you feel scattered?

These are not judgments. They are inquiries. They help the medium stay connected to their truth. They help ensure that the spiritual path remains a healing one, not another way of avoiding pain.

Some mediums may experience both states. They may begin a reading in trance and slide into dissociation if something is triggered.

They may dissociate during particularly emotional messages. This is understandable. The work is intense. But awareness makes the difference. The medium who notices their shift can take a breath. They can pause. They can ground. They can return. Over time, this becomes second nature.

The nervous system learns that it is safe to feel. Safe to open. Safe to stay connected even in intensity. This is the path of integration.

A medium who dissociates regularly may unintentionally mislead their clients. They may deliver messages that are clouded by personal trauma. They may confuse their inner fragmentation with spiritual insight. This does not mean they are dishonest.

But it does mean they need support. Supervision, therapy, and peer mentorship can help. The goal is not perfection. The goal is alignment. The more grounded the medium is, the more their clients benefit. The more integrated they are, the more clearly spirit can speak through them.

Ultimately, the difference between trance and dissociation is the difference between surrender and escape. Trance is a deepening. Dissociation is a leaving. Trance is a choice. Dissociation is a reaction. Trance brings clarity. Dissociation brings confusion.

Trance connects. Dissociation separates. To walk the path of mediumship is to become intimate with these inner landscapes. It is to know the terrain of the soul. It is to recognize when you are grounded and when you are floating. When you are present and when you are gone.

This awareness transforms everything. It brings safety. It brings power. It brings trust. The medium no longer fears the deep states. They know how to enter and how to return. They know how to hold their own hand through the mystery. They become a lighthouse, not just for others, but for themselves. This is the medicine. This is the way.

Here are 10 affirmations to help you remain grounded and integrated while facilitating trance mediumship, supporting your awareness, energetic sovereignty, and safe return:

1. I remain rooted in my body as I open to the presence of spirit.

2. My consciousness expands, but my awareness of self remains clear and intact.

3. I allow spirit to speak through me, but I do not lose myself in the process.

4. I trust my boundaries and know how to safely guide the flow of energy.

5. I am a conscious participant, not a passive vessel.

6. I release the need to leave my body in order to receive truth.

7. My nervous system is calm, supported, and fully present in this work.

8. I return to myself gently and completely after each session.

9. I am grounded in my breath, anchored in my heart, and aware of my being.

10. I honour both the spirit world and my own body as sacred, connected, and one.

34. The Witch Wound – Healing the Fear of Being Seen

Beneath the surface of many mediums, healers, psychics, and spiritually attuned souls lives a deep, often unspoken fear. It is not always logical. It may not be linked to any one experience. Yet it shows itself in hesitation, self-silencing, chronic visibility blocks, and the quiet terror that something bad will happen if they speak their truth.

This is the witch wound. It is not a metaphor. It is a soul-level imprint passed through generations, past lives, ancestral lines, and collective consciousness. It is the energetic residue of persecution, exile, shaming, torture, and death carried out against those who were once healers, seers, midwives, herbalists, and intuitives.

In times when connection to spirit was forbidden, punished, or pathologized, those with the gift learned to hide. That hiding lives on.

To understand the witch wound is to understand how fear embeds itself into the nervous system, the psyche, and the energy field. It is not only about what happened centuries ago. It is also about what continues to happen when intuition is dismissed as delusion, when empathy is pathologized, when spiritual insight is mocked, and when those who hear or see beyond the veil are told they are unstable.

The modern world may no longer burn witches at the stake, but it still punishes those who do not conform. It still rewards silence over sensitivity. It still favors logic over knowing. This creates a quiet war inside the sensitive soul. One part wants to speak. The other part remembers what happened last time.

For mediums, the witch wound often shows up in the early stages of their calling. There is a longing to serve, to be seen, to help. But alongside it comes anxiety, self-doubt, and shame. There may be dreams of being chased or silenced. There may be irrational fears of being publicly exposed. There may be chronic illness, especially in the throat or reproductive systems.

The medium may hold back, procrastinate, or sabotage opportunities to shine. They may downplay their abilities, fearing ridicule. They may experience physical symptoms such as nausea, sweating, shaking when preparing to speak about their work. These are not mere mindset issues. They are soul echoes. They are trauma responses. And they deserve sacred tending.

The witch wound is not limited to women, though it often expresses more visibly in feminine-presenting individuals due to the historic association between femininity and intuitive power.

Men, non-binary people, and others across the gender spectrum also carry this imprint. Anyone who has been persecuted for their spiritual gifts, their uniqueness, or their refusal to conform may carry the witch wound. It is an ancient wound. But it can be healed. Healing it does not mean forgetting what happened. It means remembering with compassion, reclaiming with strength, and choosing to rise anyway.

Part of healing the witch wound involves reclaiming the word witch itself. For many, this word still carries a heavy charge. It may feel dangerous or inappropriate. But at its root, the word witch was once synonymous with wise one. It was not about evil. It was about earth wisdom, lunar knowledge, herbal medicine, and spiritual connection. It was about midwives and mystics, those who understood cycles and spirits, those who listened to the land and honoured the dead.

To reclaim this heritage is not to adopt a label out of trend or rebellion. It is to stand in remembrance. To say I carry wisdom that was once feared. I carry light that was once punished. And I choose not to hide it any longer.

This reclamation is not always easy. It can stir grief, anger, and fear. It may require confronting memories that do not seem to belong to this lifetime.

Many mediums who carry the witch wound report spontaneous past-life memories of persecution. They may recall being tried, burned, drowned, or imprisoned. These memories may come in dreams, visions, regressions, or intuitive flashes.

Whether or not they can be verified historically does not matter. What matters is how they feel. The body remembers. The soul remembers. And these memories are often triggered precisely at the threshold of expansion. Just as the medium is ready to become more visible, the memory surfaces. It is not there to punish. It is there to be healed.

Healing the witch wound involves deep nervous system work. The body must learn that it is safe to be seen. Safe to speak. Safe to stand in spiritual power. This requires regulation, grounding, and compassion. Practices such as breathwork, tapping, somatic tracking, and trauma-informed movement can help discharge the fear stored in the body.

Affirmations are not enough. The healing must be felt. The medium must build a relationship of trust with their own body. They must learn the difference between real danger and historical imprint. They must learn to stay present with discomfort instead of retreating into hiding.

Energetically, the witch wound may show up as blockages in the throat chakra, solar plexus, or sacral region. These centres govern expression, power, and creativity. When the wound is active, the throat may feel tight. Words may get stuck. The stomach may churn with anxiety. The sacral area may hold guilt or suppression.

Healing these centres involves not just clearing but reclaiming. The medium must find their voice. They must speak even when the voice shakes. They must name their truth. Not for validation, but for liberation.

One of the most sacred rituals for healing the witch wound is ancestral dialogue. The medium may create space to speak with their lineage, both biological and spiritual. They may ask, What did you have to hide? What gifts did you bury? What pain did you carry in silence? What wisdom do you want me to reclaim?

This dialogue is not about blame. It is about connection. Many of our ancestors were not allowed to express their spiritual nature. They were bound by culture, religion, or fear. They may not have had the tools or language we now possess. By healing ourselves, we heal them. By speaking now, we speak for those who could not.

The witch wound also creates community wounds. It teaches mediums to isolate, to mistrust others, to fear spiritual groups. This isolation is both emotional and energetic. The medium may long for connection but fear betrayal. They may have been hurt by previous spiritual communities. They may have witnessed power used abusively and now hesitate to belong anywhere. This fear of belonging must also be healed.

No one heals alone. The witch was never meant to be solitary. The lone witch archetype is a trauma response. Historically, many who carried spiritual gifts worked in community. They shared wisdom, supported birth and death, celebrated seasons together.

Healing this wound means reclaiming healthy spiritual community. It means choosing spaces that honour sovereignty, consent, and authenticity. It means risking trust again.

Shame is at the heart of the witch wound. The shame of being different. The shame of being intuitive. The shame of having emotions that run deep. The shame of knowing things others cannot explain. This shame must be named to be released.

The medium must speak it aloud. I was taught to hide. I was told I was wrong. I was made to feel dangerous. These truths, once named, begin to lose their power. Shame thrives in silence. It dissolves in compassion. The medium must offer themselves the compassion that history did not.

There is also a modern witch wound, one created not by fire and gallows, but by the subtle violence of scepticism, ridicule, and spiritual commodification. Mediums today still face the fear of being seen as frauds, fakes, or unstable. They may be mocked by family, dismissed by friends, or attacked online.

This creates a double bind. Speak and risk harm. Stay silent and suffocate. Healing the modern witch wound means reclaiming spiritual authority. It means standing in the truth that lived experience is valid. That intuition is intelligence. That spirit connection is not delusion. The medium must learn to take up space—not with arrogance, but with grounded conviction.

One of the final stages of witch wound healing is embodiment. This is when the medium stops explaining and simply lives their truth. They stop defending their gift. They start walking in it. They allow themselves to be seen as they are.

This does not mean reckless exposure. It means conscious presence. It means choosing to be visible without apology. It means saying yes to life, yes to voice, yes to path. This embodiment is magnetic. It invites others to rise. It creates a field of permission. It turns the wound into wisdom.

Healing the witch wound is not a one-time process. It is layered, cyclical, and sacred. It is not just personal. It is collective. Every time a medium chooses to be seen, to speak truth, to stand in integrity, they help dismantle the energy of persecution. They create a new imprint in the field. One of safety. One of power. One of love.

There is a reason the witch wound is reawakening now. Humanity is remembering. The veils are thinning. The need for spiritual truth-tellers is growing. But for the message to be pure, the vessel must be free. Free from shame. Free from silence. Free from the chains of memory that no longer serve. The world does not need perfect mediums. It needs honest ones. Brave ones. Embodied ones. Those who have met their fear and walked through it. Those who carry not just messages, but medicine.

You were never wrong to feel. You were never wrong to know. You were never wrong to speak. The world tried to make you forget because your remembering is powerful. But your soul never forgot. And now it is time to rise. To speak. To serve. Not in hiding, but in honour. The witch is not a threat. The witch is a healer. The medium is not lost. The medium is a messenger, and your voice once silenced, now becomes the sound of freedom.

Reflection Questions: The Witch Wound – Healing the Fear of Being Seen

1. What does being "seen" in my spiritual truth stir within me, pride, fear, shame, or a mixture of all?

2. Where in my body do I feel tension or resistance when I step forward publicly in my gifts?

3. What ancestral or cultural memories might I carry around the danger of being intuitive, powerful, or outspoken?

4. Have I ever silenced myself to stay safe, from judgment, rejection, or spiritual persecution?

5. What would it look like to express my full spiritual self without apology or fear of consequence?

6. Who in my lineage, past lives, or soul memory tried to speak and was silenced, and how can I honour them by using my voice now?

7. If I truly believed that visibility was not a threat but a blessing, how would I begin showing up differently in my work, life, and spiritual path?

35. Illness as Initiation – When the Body Becomes the Messenger

There is a moment that comes quietly or violently when the body says no. It may come as a whisper in the bones, a burning in the chest, a sudden collapse of strength. It may take the form of chronic fatigue, autoimmune conditions, heart attacks, unexplained pain, or a slow unravelling of systems once taken for granted. In that moment, everything stops.

The noise of the outer world dims and the body demands presence. For the medium, the healer, the empathic, and the spiritual seeker, this is not just a physical crisis. It is a call to initiation. The illness that arrives is not always an enemy. Sometimes, it is the gatekeeper to a deeper truth. Sometimes, it is the body becoming the voice of the soul.

Illness as initiation is an ancient concept. In indigenous cultures around the world, the shaman was often chosen not by bloodline or ambition, but by crisis. A sudden illness, near-death experience, or spiritual affliction would mark the beginning of their training.

It was understood that such a threshold was not a punishment but a calling. The body became the site of transformation. The person who emerged from that descent was never the same. They carried medicine not only for themselves, but for the community. In modern times, this sacred framing of illness has been largely forgotten.

We are taught to fear the body when it breaks, to suppress symptoms, to silence pain. But for those on the spiritual path, illness often brings with it a hidden invitation.

The medium's body is the vessel through which spirit speaks. When that vessel begins to falter, the medium is often forced to listen more deeply than ever before. The messages may no longer come from guides or visions. They may come from the cells. From the breath. From the slow ache that cannot be ignored. Illness strips away the distractions. It dismantles the illusion of control. It humbles. It quiets. It places the medium face to face with mortality, vulnerability, and the reality that the spiritual path must include the body or it is not whole.

The body is not a barrier to spiritual work. It is the container. The partner. The oracle.

Illness can arrive as a reckoning. A culmination of years of spiritual bypassing, emotional repression, over giving, or energetic depletion. The medium who constantly serves others while ignoring their own needs may find their body beginning to shut down.

The one who suppresses grief, avoids shadow, or denies rest may awaken one day to find that the body will no longer cooperate. This is not a failure. It is a sacred pause. It is the soul's way of saying it is time to come home. It is time to listen. It is time to heal not only others, but the self.

There are many layers to illness. The physical layer is real and must be honoured. Diagnosis, treatment, medication, and medical care are not signs of spiritual weakness. They are acts of self-respect.

But beneath the physical often lies the emotional, the ancestral, the karmic, and the spiritual. A chronic illness may carry within it the grief of generations. An autoimmune condition may reflect an internal war, the body attacking itself just as the psyche attacks its own sensitivity.

A heart condition may point to old heartbreaks never fully processed. The body remembers what the mind forgets. It stores trauma. It echoes soul patterns. It speaks the language of sensation, asking us to pay attention.

Mediums who fall ill often report an increase in spiritual sensitivity. As the body becomes more fragile, the veil thins. Dreams become more vivid. Visitations from spirit become more frequent. The inner voice becomes louder. This is not a coincidence. The body, in its brokenness, opens the gateway to deeper listening. The ego softens. The distractions fall away. What remains is raw truth.

In this space, the medium is remade. Not through striving, but through surrender. Not by achieving, but by allowing.

One of the hardest parts of illness as initiation is the isolation. Friends may drift away. The work may stop. The roles the medium once held may dissolve. In this empty space, identity crumbles. The question arises: who am I when I can no longer perform, provide, or produce? This is the heart of the initiation. The old self dies. The masks fall. The medium is stripped bare, returned to the essence of being. This is where the true work begins. This is where the soul begins to speak not in channellings or messages, but in stillness. In breath. In pain that becomes a prayer.

There is also rage. The body that once served so well now feels like a prison. There is grief for what has been lost. There is fear of what lies ahead. These emotions are not to be bypassed. They are to be honoured. They are sacred. They are part of the initiation. The illness asks, can you hold yourself in your weakness? Can you find divinity in your limits? Can you serve from stillness, receive without guilt, and remember that you are not what you do, but who you are?

Illness may also carry spiritual purpose beyond the personal.

The medium who has walked through the fire of their own suffering becomes a more compassionate channel. They understand the pain of others more deeply. Their readings take on new depth. Their energy carries the vibration of survival, of truth earned not from books but from the body. They become living medicine. Not because they are healed, but because they are healing.

Not because they have answers, but because they know how to sit in the unknown.

The ego resists this. It wants to be strong, visible, in control. It does not want to be vulnerable. But the soul knows that vulnerability is the path to authenticity.

When illness comes, it shatters the illusions of power. It brings the medium into alignment with their humanity. And in that humanity, spirit finds a more honest channel. The messages become softer, truer.

The medium no longer speaks from performance, but from presence. They know what it means to lose, to ache, to wait in the darkness for a light that may never come. And when they speak, others listen, not because of what they say, but because of who they have become.

There is a grief that comes when the life you knew is no longer possible. The plans you made are no longer feasible. The body you trusted now moves slowly, painfully.

But this grief is sacred. It is the mourning of an identity that has outlived its usefulness. It is the letting go of striving, of proving, of pretending. It is the return to soul. To essence. To the one within who has always been whole, even when the body is not.

For mediums navigating illness, the spiritual path does not end. It changes. It deepens. It slows. The practices may shift from long ceremonies to moments of breath. The offerings may shift from public readings to quiet prayers. The visibility may wane, but the potency increases.

The medium learns that they are still of service even in stillness. They are still a vessel even when bedridden. Spirit does not need performance. Spirit needs presence. Illness becomes a teacher, not of suffering alone, but of grace. Of softness. Of truth.

Community is essential during this initiation. The medium must not be left alone. They need support that honours both the spiritual and the physical. They need doctors who listen, friends who stay, and mentors who understand that illness does not disqualify spiritual work. It deepens it. They need space to rage, to cry, to question, to rest. And most importantly, they need to be reminded that their worth is not based on output. Their medicine is in their being.

As recovery begins, whether full or partial, the medium emerges changed. Slower. Wiser. More tender. They carry new boundaries, deeper self-respect, and a clarity that can only be forged in fire. They no longer tolerate what drains them. They no longer chase what is not aligned. They become guardians of their own energy. They learn to say no without guilt. They learn to say yes with reverence. Their work becomes more honest. Their words more grounded. Their presence more healing.

Not all illness ends in recovery. Some remain chronic. Some become terminal. The medium who walks this path carries medicine for us all. They teach us how to live with grace even in decline. How to listen even when the noise of pain is loud. How to serve with presence, not perfection. They remind us that spirit does not abandon the body when it breaks. Spirit enters more deeply. Spirit sits beside us on the hospital bed. Spirit walks with us into the unknown.

To see illness as initiation is not to romanticize suffering. It is to reclaim it as sacred. It is to find meaning in what may feel meaningless. It is to let the body become a temple, even when it is trembling. The body does not betray us. It speaks for us when we cannot. It says what the soul has long been whispering.

It asks us to come home. To rest. To remember and in that remembering, we are reborn, not as who we were, but as who we truly are.

Reflection Questions: Illness as Initiation – When the Body Becomes the Messenger

1. What was happening emotionally, spiritually, or energetically in my life before my body became unwell?

2. In what ways has illness slowed me down, redirected me, or initiated a deeper connection with my soul?

3. What unspoken truths or suppressed feelings might my body have been trying to bring to light?

4. Have I treated my body as a battleground, or as a sacred messenger trying to communicate with me?

5. How did illness change the way I relate to spirit, intuition, and my purpose as a medium?

6. What grief have I carried in my body that words could not express?

7. How do I feel when I allow myself to rest, receive, and surrender, rather than push, perform, or prove?

8. Have I ever experienced shame, blame, or spiritual bypassing in response to my illness and what healing did I need in those moments?

9. What parts of me became more alive, wise, or spiritually attuned through the experience of being unwell?

10. What has my pain taught me about compassion for others and how has it changed the way I hold space as a medium?

11. What limiting beliefs about strength, independence, or worth surfaced when I had to rely on others?

12. If I saw my body as a sacred vessel instead of something broken or betraying me, what would shift in my healing journey?

13. What message is my body still whispering to me today and am I finally ready to listen?

36. Navigating Ethical Dilemmas in Mediumship

In the sacred work of mediumship, ethics is not a side note. It is the foundation.

Every reading, message, trance, or communication with spirit exists within a moral and energetic framework. While much focus is placed on the development of skills, the refinement of clair abilities, and the expansion of spiritual awareness, it is ethics that truly defines a medium's integrity.

A gifted medium without ethics is dangerous. An ethical medium without gifts can still bring healing. The work is powerful. It reaches into the depths of grief, trauma, hope, and identity. With that power comes responsibility. And with responsibility comes the inevitable encounter with ethical dilemmas, that those grey areas where answers are not always clear, and choices must be made with discernment, humility, and heart.

Ethical dilemmas in mediumship are not rare. They arise in almost every aspect of practice. They emerge in client relationships, in the interpretation of messages, in the delivery of difficult truths, and in the boundaries between the medium's personal beliefs and the needs of those they serve.

These dilemmas are not necessarily signs of failure. They are opportunities to refine one's practice. They are invitations to deeper self-awareness. They ask the medium to pause, to reflect, and to remember that their role is not to impress, to control, or to dominate, but to serve as a clear, compassionate channel for healing and truth.

One of the most common ethical dilemmas in mediumship concerns the delivery of painful or sensitive information. A medium may receive a message about a past trauma, an infidelity, an illness, or even a potential death. The question arises: should this be shared? And if so, how?

Ethics in mediumship does not require brutal honesty. It requires compassionate honesty. The medium must ask not only is this true, but is this helpful? Is this timely? Is the client ready to receive this? Am I the right person to deliver it? These questions cannot always be answered with certainty, but they must be asked.

The goal is not to withhold, but to honour the dignity and emotional safety of the person in front of you.

Another ethical challenge involves spiritual boundaries. A medium may be asked to read for someone who has not given consent. For example, a client may request insight into a partner, an ex-lover, a boss, or a family member. The spirit world may offer impressions, but the medium must decide whether to proceed.

Reading without permission violates the energetic autonomy of another soul. It crosses into spiritual voyeurism. The medium must explain that while spirit may sometimes bring in relevant connections to those around the client, the intention must always be healing, not curiosity, control, or invasion. Just as we would not break into someone's home, we do not enter their energy without invitation.

One of the more subtle ethical dilemmas is the temptation to overidentify with the message or the client. The medium may feel emotionally pulled into the client's story. They may begin to project their own experiences, beliefs, or wounds into the reading. They may offer advice that goes beyond the scope of spirit communication and drifts into counselling, therapy, or life coaching.

While it is natural for a medium to care deeply, they must also remain clear about their role. They are not therapists unless trained to be so. They are not saviours. They are not responsible for the choices their clients make. They are messengers. Guides. Witnesses. Their work is to illuminate, not to direct.

There is also the ethical question of prediction. Many clients come seeking answers about the future; will I meet someone, will I get the job, will I recover, will they come back? While spirit may offer insights, the future is not fixed.

Mediums must be honest about this. Every message is shaped by energy, and energy can shift. The ethical medium resists the urge to offer certainty where none exists. They speak of possibilities, not promises. They empower the client to participate in their own destiny, rather than placing all power in external messages. When handled carelessly, predictions can disempower, create anxiety, or lead to dependency.

When handled ethically, they inspire reflection, not fear.

Dependency is another major ethical concern. A client who becomes overly reliant on mediumship may begin to seek constant readings, delaying decisions until they receive guidance, and outsourcing their inner knowing. This creates a spiritual imbalance.

The medium must recognize when this pattern is forming and gently guide the client back to self-trust. This may mean encouraging time between sessions, referring to other forms of support, or even declining further readings if the relationship becomes unhealthy. Mediumship is meant to awaken autonomy, not create addiction.

The ethical medium knows when to step back. They do not use fear or manipulation to keep clients returning. They do not claim exclusive access to the divine.

The medium's personal energy and well-being are also part of the ethical equation. Burnout, unresolved trauma, or emotional depletion can distort the messages received and delivered.

A medium who is ungrounded, sick, or energetically compromised is more prone to misinterpretation, projection, or reactivity. Self-care is not selfish. It is sacred preparation. The medium has an ethical duty to themselves to maintain spiritual hygiene, emotional balance, and clear boundaries.

This includes saying no to readings when they are not in alignment. It includes being honest about limitations. The ethical medium does not perform at the expense of their health. They know that being a clear channel requires clarity of being.

Another ethical consideration is how the medium presents their work to the public. In a world of social media and spiritual marketing, the line between authentic sharing and exaggerated promotion can become blurred.

The ethical medium is transparent. They do not promise miracles. They do not prey on grief. They do not claim to remove curses, reunite lost lovers, or offer spiritual services in exchange for loyalty or secrecy. They respect the intelligence and dignity of their audience. They speak with integrity. Their offerings are based on service, not seduction. They allow their work to speak for itself, without resorting to fear-based tactics.

There are also ethical challenges related to cultural sensitivity and appropriation. Mediums must be aware of the origins of the practices they use, the cultures they draw from, and the communities they represent. They must ask whether they have the right, training, or permission to use certain rituals, symbols, or terminology. Spirituality does not exist in a vacuum. It is rooted in history, ancestry, and context.

The ethical medium honours this. They acknowledge where their practices come from. They listen to those whose traditions they engage with. They do not exploit or romanticize. They walk with humility.

Mediums also face ethical questions in public demonstrations or group readings. When reading for multiple people at once, how much information is appropriate to share? What if a message is deeply personal or involves trauma?

The ethical medium sets clear expectations before beginning. They obtain consent. They create safe containers. They allow people to opt out or receive messages privately. The goal is never entertainment. It is always healing.

The medium is not a performer. They are a steward of sacred moments. They must be prepared to hold space for emotion, boundaries, and complex human dynamics.

Mediums may also encounter spirit beings who offer messages that are unclear, confronting, or emotionally charged.

The medium must then discern whether to share the message as received, soften it, or withhold it entirely. This is not censorship. It is discernment. Spirit communication is a delicate art. Not every message must be delivered exactly as it arrives.

The medium is not a robot. They are a human translator. Their job is to honour both the spirit and the client. This sometimes means editing for clarity, context, and kindness. The ethical medium asks, what is the deeper truth here? What is the message behind the message? What serves the greatest good?

There is also the question of mediumship and grief.

Many clients come in deep mourning, longing for connection with lost loved ones. The ethical medium meets this with tenderness. They do not rush. They do not make promises. They do not use grief to create urgency or dependency. They offer space. Presence. Permission to feel.

They help the client reconnect not only with the spirit of the departed, but with their own inner resilience. They understand that grief is not a problem to be solved, but a process to be witnessed. They do not claim to fix the pain. They walk beside it.

In all of these dilemmas, the core question remains the same—what serves healing? What honours both the client and the spirit? What upholds the sacredness of this work?

The answers will vary. There is no single ethical code that fits every situation. But there are guiding principles: respect, consent, transparency, humility, and compassion. These are the true tools of the ethical medium. Without them, the work becomes hollow, even harmful. With them, the work becomes transformational.

Ethical reflection is not a one-time checklist. It is an ongoing practice. The ethical medium engages in supervision, mentorship, and inner inquiry. They admit when they are wrong. They learn from mistakes. They listen to feedback. They remain students of their own growth. They do not use spirituality as a shield for ego or control. They understand that the more power one holds, the more accountability is required.

Mediumship is sacred. It touches the soul, the heart, the unseen. It must be held with reverence. Ethics is not a limitation. It is a liberation. It frees the medium from confusion, guilt, and fear. It creates safety. It builds trust. It ensures that the messages delivered are not only accurate but aligned.

The ethical medium becomes a lighthouse in a chaotic world and a presence of peace, clarity, and truth.

In that space, miracles can happen. Not because of showmanship, but because of sincerity. Not because of grand claims, but because of gentle truth.

The ethical medium does not need to prove. They need only to be. To show up with presence. To speak with care. To listen with the whole heart. To serve with love.

37. When Spirit Goes Quiet – Trusting the Silence in Mediumship

There comes a time in every medium's journey when the voices fade. The familiar sensations of presence dissolve. The once constant flow of impressions, images, whispers, and insights slows or even stops entirely. A stillness settles in, vast and unnerving.

This is not a lack of ability.

This is not punishment.

This is not failure.

This is the silence. And it is one of the most misunderstood aspects of the mediumship path. For many, it is also the most painful. To serve spirit, to open oneself daily to the unseen, to walk between worlds with devotion, and then suddenly to be met with nothing can feel like abandonment. It can shake the very foundations of purpose and identity. But the silence, if understood correctly, is not a void.

It is a sacred space. A teacher. A purification. A calling inward.

The silence arrives in many ways. Sometimes it follows a great period of expansion. The medium may have been giving powerful readings, receiving vivid messages, feeling deeply attuned to spirit and then, without warning, it all goes quiet.

Other times, the silence comes after a life change. A loss. An illness. A trauma. A spiritual awakening. The sensitivity remains, but the signals seem jammed. There are also those who experience the silence as a part of seasonal or cyclical rhythm. Just as the earth has its winters, so too does the spiritual path. The question becomes not how to make the silence go away, but how to be with it. How to trust it. How to allow it to do its work.

For mediums, silence can provoke panic. Have I lost my gift? Am I being punished? Am I doing something wrong? These thoughts are natural. But they are rarely true. The silence is not an erasure of the gift. It is a refinement. Spirit never leaves. But the way spirit communicates may shift.

Sometimes the silence is not on their end but on ours. The noise of life, stress, ego, fear, and emotional exhaustion can drown out subtle impressions. In those moments, spirit waits. Not with judgment, but with compassion. They know the path is long. They know the vessel must be tended.

There are also times when the silence is divinely orchestrated. Spirit steps back to allow the medium to grow. To deepen. To reclaim the self-outside the work. To grieve. To rest. To realign.

In a world that values output, silence feels like failure. But in the spiritual world, silence is often preparation. The ground is being cleared.

The old ways of connecting may no longer be aligned. The messages that once flowed easily may have served their season. Something new is forming. But first, space must be made.

Many mediums try to push through the silence. They meditate harder. They call in spirit more forcefully. They take more clients. They worry. They question. They compare. But the silence cannot be forced open. It is not a wall. It is a womb. It is not a door closed in rejection. It is an invitation to soften, to listen with new ears.

The most powerful way to move through the silence is to surrender to it. To let it teach. To let it rearrange what must be rearranged. Spirit is not punishing you. Spirit is inviting you to become more attuned, not just to them, but to yourself.

The silence often reveals what has been hidden beneath the work. Without the constant stream of messages, the medium must confront their own thoughts, wounds, and needs. They may discover how much of their identity was tied to being a channel.

They may feel lost without the flow of validation, service, or spiritual contact. This is part of the healing. The silence asks: who are you when you are not being useful? Who are you without the voices? What parts of you have you neglected in your devotion to the unseen?

This can bring grief. The medium may feel abandoned not just by spirit but by purpose. But grief is not emptiness. It is love with nowhere to go. And in that grief is the medicine. The medium is called to return to themselves. To nourish their body. To tend to their nervous system. To rest. To breathe. To feel.

These are not distractions from the path. They are the path. The silence is the rebalancing of a system that has been overextended. The vessel must be whole, not just open. The spirit world needs you well. Not just active.

Sometimes the silence reveals new gifts. When the usual senses are quiet, other channels begin to awaken.

A medium who relied on clairaudience may begin to feel more through clairsentience. A visual channel may develop stronger knowing. The silence reshapes the way spirit flows. It refines the edges. It brings subtlety. What once felt like absence may become a softer, more integrated presence.

The spirit world is not always loud. Sometimes it is a breath on the skin. A tug at the heart. A dream that lingers. The medium learns to listen with the whole self.

The silence also teaches boundaries. Many mediums become so accustomed to being open that they forget to close. They become energetically porous, always listening, always giving, always attuned to the unseen. This can lead to burnout, confusion, and exhaustion. The silence forces a pause. It creates a sacred container. It reminds the medium that they are not a faucet to be left running. They are a sacred vessel.

They get to choose when to open and when to rest. The silence is the reset button. It returns the power of consent.

In the silence, the medium may also encounter their own soul more clearly. Without the noise of messages, they can hear their own inner voice. Their own desires. Their own needs.

Sometimes spirit steps back so the medium can hear themselves. The most powerful readings come not just from connection to the spirit world, but from deep self-awareness. The silence cultivates this. It is a mirror. It reflects back what has been buried beneath the work.

There may also be a shift in spiritual resonance. The medium who once connected with certain guides, beings, or realms may find those connections fading. This is not abandonment. It is graduation. The guides who have walked with you have served their purpose. Others are waiting.

But first, space must be made. The silence is the in-between. It is the cocoon. What feels like death may be transformation. But transformation cannot be rushed.

The medium must learn to honour the silence not as a punishment, but as a phase. Like the moon, like the tides, like the breath. It comes and it goes. In its stillness, there is wisdom. In its quiet, there is depth. In its space, there is preparation for what is next.

The greatest spiritual breakthroughs often follow the deepest silences. The soul needs time to catch up. The ego needs time to let go. The body needs time to integrate.

For those walking through the silence now, know this: you are not broken. You are not lost. You are not alone. Spirit is still with you. But they are whispering now, not shouting. They are asking you to listen in a new way. To trust the unseen. To trust yourself.

The silence is not absence. It is presence in a different form.

Write. Walk. Rest. Breathe. Let the silence speak. Let it teach you to hold space not only for others, but for yourself. You are still a medium, even when the messages are not flowing. You are still a bridge, even when both shores are hidden in fog. This is the work behind the work. This is the sacred pause before the sacred return.

When the voices return, as they often do, they will come into a vessel more grounded, more clear, more true. The messages will be richer. The connection more stable. The medium more humble. More embodied. More whole. The silence will not have broken the gift. It will have strengthened it. Refined it. Deepened it.

You will remember that even when spirit goes quiet, love does not. Connection does not. Your worth does not. The gift is not what makes you valuable. Your being is. And that is enough. Always.

Reflection Questions: When Spirit Goes Quiet – Trusting the Silence in Mediumship

1. What emotions rise within me when spirit feels distant or silent, fear, doubt, abandonment, or stillness?

2. Do I believe that silence means something is wrong with me, or could it be an invitation into deeper trust?

3. How do I respond to the silence, do I push harder, withdraw, question myself, or allow space for mystery?

4. Have I internalised the idea that mediumship must always be "on" or productive in order to be valid?

5. What patterns from my childhood or past experiences might influence how I react to spiritual quietness?

6. Can I sit with the unknown without needing to fill it, emotionally, psychically, or energetically?

7. What part of me still seeks constant reassurance from spirit instead of cultivating inner steadiness?

8. In what ways could silence be a sacred pause for integration, rest, or healing?

9. Have I confused spiritual silence with rejection or failure and what would it take to reframe that belief?

10. What is spirit teaching me about patience, presence, or self-trust in this quiet season?

11. When I honour silence as part of the cycle of connection, how does that shift the pressure I place on myself?

12. What other senses or intuitive faculties become more alive when the "voice" of spirit goes quiet?

13. Have I ever received my most profound wisdom not in words, but in silence?

14. How might spirit be encouraging me to rely less on them and more on my own inner knowing?

15. Do I need to grieve a part of my identity that was tied to always being "connected" in order to become more whole?

16. Could the silence be a sign that I am being prepared for a deeper kind of mediumship I cannot yet understand?

17. How does stillness in mediumship mirror stillness in nature, death, or the void, can I find beauty in it?

38. Sacred Listening – Becoming the Vessel, Not the Voice

Mediumship is often associated with speaking. It is seen as a transmission. A gift of verbal communication. A voice that relays messages from the unseen to the living. But at the heart of mediumship lies something even more essential than speech. That essence is sacred listening. Long before words form, long before a message is delivered, there is a silence filled with presence. It is in that silence that true connection is made. The greatest mediums are not those who speak the most or dazzle with detail.

They are those who listen with their whole being. They listen with the body, with the soul, with the heart, with the nervous system, and with reverence. To become a true vessel, the medium must master the art of listening. Not just hearing. Listening.

Sacred listening is not passive. It is an active, intentional state of presence. It requires the medium to empty themselves of distraction, judgment, and expectation. It is not about waiting to respond. It is about becoming so still, so receptive, that even the faintest impression is felt.

This level of listening begins in the self. Before a medium can truly listen to spirit, they must learn to listen to their own energy. This includes their emotions, sensations, thoughts, and intuitive pulses. If the inner world is noisy, confused, or scattered, the messages received will be distorted. Sacred listening means becoming a clear vessel.

Not a perfect one, but a conscious one.

The difference between being the vessel and being the voice is subtle but significant. When a medium tries to be the voice, they may take ownership of the message. They may feel pressure to perform, to deliver on expectations, to prove their ability. The ego gets involved.

The medium may unintentionally insert their own opinions, fears, or desires into the communication. But when a medium surrenders to being the vessel, they allow the message to come through them, not from them. They hold space without interfering. They become the riverbed, not the water. The message flows through, not because of them, but because they are willing to hold it.

Becoming a vessel requires humility. The medium must accept that they are not the source of the message. They are the conduit. The cleaner the conduit, the clearer the message. This is not about disappearing or erasing the self. It is about aligning with something larger. The medium does not disappear. They become more integrated. More grounded. More able to discern what is theirs and what belongs to spirit.

Sacred listening helps create this discernment. It teaches the medium to know their own voice so clearly that they can recognize when another voice enters.

Listening to spirit is not always about hearing words. Messages come in many forms; sensations, emotions, images, smells, sudden knowing's, or shifts in energy. The medium must learn to listen with all senses. The body becomes a receiver.

The skin becomes sensitive to temperature changes. The stomach becomes a truth detector. The heart picks up grief. The throat tightens with urgency. Every part of the medium becomes a listening device.

Sacred listening means paying attention to these subtleties. It means trusting them, even when they defy logic.

Listening also requires spaciousness. In a fast-paced world, the act of slowing down to receive is revolutionary. The medium must create space before, during, and after communication. This space is where the message forms. It is the pause between the breath. The stillness between questions. It is where meaning deepens.

Many mediums rush through the experience, eager to impress or fill silence. But spirit often speaks in layers. If the medium can wait, can sit in the discomfort of quiet, more will be revealed. Sacred listening is not about speed. It is about depth.

Sacred listening extends to the client as well. Too often, mediums focus solely on what spirit says and forget to deeply listen to the living person in front of them. The client brings their own energy, story, and emotions into the space. They may not say everything out loud, but they are communicating. Their body language, tone, and silence speak volumes. The ethical medium listens to all of it. They hold space for the client's truth, not just spirit's. In doing so, the reading becomes a conversation, not a performance.

The client feels seen, not just told. The medium becomes a mirror, not a pedestal.

Listening is also essential in the relationship with guides. Spirit guides have unique ways of communicating. Some are direct. Others are symbolic. Some use emotions. Others speak through signs.

The medium must learn how each guide speaks and be willing to listen beyond words. This is a relationship built over time. The more the medium listens, the clearer the guidance becomes. Not because the guides are louder, but because the medium is quieter. Sacred listening means creating consistent space for connection, even when no messages are needed. It means showing up not just to ask for help, but to be in communion.

There are times when listening requires the medium to sit with discomfort. Spirit may bring through messages that are difficult, emotional, or unexpected. The medium may feel overwhelmed, unsure, or resistant. Sacred listening means staying present anyway. It means not editing or judging the message too quickly. It means listening long enough to understand the deeper purpose behind what is being shared.

This takes courage. It takes self-trust. And it takes the willingness to be a student, even in the middle of a reading.

The process of listening is also affected by the medium's inner world. If the medium is carrying unresolved trauma, grief, or fear, it will affect what they hear. Sacred listening includes inner healing. The clearer the medium's own emotional landscape, the more accurately they can perceive spirit. This is not about being healed completely.

It is about being honest about where healing is needed. It is about creating an inner environment that supports receptivity rather than distortion.

There is also a deeper layer to sacred listening. Beyond clients, beyond spirit, beyond guides, there is the soul of the medium themselves. The soul speaks in longings, in fatigue, in bursts of creativity, in dreams, in resistance. Sacred listening means paying attention to what your own soul is asking of you.

It means not using mediumship as an escape. It means remembering that your soul's voice matters too. This voice will tell you when to rest. When to say no. When to change direction. When to grow. It is the compass beneath all the messages. If the medium loses touch with their own soul, the work becomes empty.

Listening to spirit must include listening to self.

Sacred listening is a devotional act. It is an act of love. It says to the spirit world, I respect you enough to wait. I trust you enough to be still. I honour this enough to open without agenda. It says to the client, I am here with you, not just for you. I see you. I hear you. I value you. It says to the self, I am willing to hear the truth. Even when it is hard. Even when it asks me to change.

In practical terms, sacred listening can be cultivated through ritual.

Before each reading, the medium may light a candle, take a breath, place a hand on their heart, and say silently, I am here. I am listening. I am open. After each reading, they may take a moment to reflect. What did I hear? What did I feel? Where did I hesitate? Where did I trust? These practices deepen the listening. They build trust over time. They remind the medium that every reading is not just an act of speaking but of receiving.

The world needs more listeners. Not just talkers. Not just teachers. But those who are willing to sit in the silence with another soul. Mediums have a unique gift. They hear what others cannot. But the true gift is not the hearing. It is the listening. The quiet, grounded, sacred presence that allows healing to happen. That presence is rare and it is powerful.

To be a vessel is to say yes to humility. Yes to spaciousness. Yes to the unknown. It is to surrender the need to be right, impressive, or certain. It is to show up with an open heart and trust that whatever needs to come will come. The voice may carry the message, but it is listening that births it. It is listening that holds it. It is listening that transforms it into medicine.

The greatest mediums are not always the loudest. They are not the ones with the flashiest visions or the most followers. They are the ones who listen. Who bow their heads before the message. Who hold space without interruption. Who trust that spirit knows what is needed, and that their job is not to speak over that wisdom, but to allow it room to breathe.

In the end, sacred listening is what connects the seen and the unseen. The human and the spirit. The soul and the world. It is the bridge. The opening. The thread of grace.

When the medium becomes that, when they embody that level of presence, they do not just deliver messages. They become the message.

Reflection Questions: Sacred Listening – Becoming the Vessel, Not the Voice

1. Do I listen with the intention to understand or with the urgency to respond?

2. When I sit with spirit, am I open to receive all messages or only those I want or expect to hear?

3. How do I know when I am fully present with someone's soul rather than interpreting through my own lens?

4. What internal noise, fear, or belief often gets in the way of truly hearing what spirit or the sitter is trying to share?

5. Have I mistaken the act of "delivering a message" for the deeper call to witness, hold, and honour another's story?

6. What practices help me empty myself enough to become a clear vessel for spirit—without agenda, ego, or interference?

7. Can I sit with silence during a session and allow something sacred to unfold, without rushing to fill the space?

8. How do I respond when I don't receive anything clearly, do I trust the silence as part of the listening process?

9. What parts of my own story make it difficult to listen objectively, and how can I continue to heal those places?

10. In what ways do I listen with my body, emotions, and spirit, not just with my mind?

11. Am I willing to hear the uncomfortable truths from spirit, even when they challenge my beliefs or comfort zone?

12. What would it mean to become a true vessel, where spirit's truth is honoured more than my performance or need to be right?

13. How can I bring more reverence, stillness, and humility into my practice of listening, so that I become not just a channel, but a sanctuary?

39. Trauma-Informed Mediumship – Holding Space for the Wounded Soul

Mediumship is not simply the art of delivering messages from the spirit world. It is a form of deep soul witnessing, and many of those who seek readings are carrying hidden wounds, unresolved grief, and layers of pain that reach far beneath the surface of their questions. To be a medium in today's world requires more than spiritual sensitivity. It requires emotional maturity. It requires psychological insight. It requires trauma awareness.

Mediums are not therapists, but they hold a power that can heal or harm. Without a trauma-informed lens, even the most well-intentioned reading can reopen wounds, retraumatize a client, or misinterpret the deeper needs behind a message. A trauma-informed approach to mediumship is not an added bonus. It is essential.

Trauma is not always visible. It lives in the nervous system, in the body, in the soul. It can be the result of obvious events like abuse, neglect, or loss. But it can also stem from years of subtle dismissal, gaslighting, identity erasure, cultural oppression, and spiritual betrayal.

Many people who come to mediums are navigating these layers of trauma, often silently. They may not say, I have trauma, but their energy speaks it. Their questions are shaped by it. Their emotional reactions are woven with it. They are not just looking for messages from beyond. They are looking to be seen. To be understood. To be held without judgment.

A trauma-informed medium begins with presence. Before any words are spoken, the way a medium holds space matters. Their tone, their body language, their energy, and their pace all contribute to the sense of safety. People who carry trauma are hyper-aware of cues. They notice subtle signs of dismissal or aggression. They sense when someone is impatient or performative.

A trauma-informed medium slows down. They meet the client with gentleness. They explain what to expect. They invite questions. They do not rush into the message. They honour the moment. They remember that for many, just sitting in front of a medium is a brave and vulnerable act.

Consent is a core part of trauma-informed practice. A medium must never assume what a person is ready to receive. Just because spirit presents a message does not mean it must be delivered immediately or in full detail. The ethical medium checks in. They ask, are you comfortable hearing about this? They pause when emotions rise. They offer choice. They explain that the client can stop the session at any time. This does not weaken the reading. It strengthens it. It tells the client, you are in control. Your agency matters. Your boundaries will be respected.

Language is another important aspect. Trauma survivors often carry internalized shame. The wrong words can reinforce that shame, even unintentionally.

A trauma-informed medium chooses language carefully. They avoid blaming, diagnosing, or spiritualizing pain in a way that bypasses human emotion. They do not say things like you attracted this or this is your karma without deep discernment.

Even if these ideas hold spiritual meaning, they must be handled with nuance. The goal is not to explain suffering but to hold it with care.

The medium does not need to fix the pain. They need to witness it with compassion.

Trauma also affects memory, perception, and interpretation. A person may forget details of the reading or react in ways that seem disproportionate. The medium does not take this personally. They understand that trauma responses are not about disrespect or dismissal. They are about protection.

The client may dissociate, shut down, or become overly compliant. A trauma-informed medium recognizes these patterns and adjusts. They ground the energy. They breathe slowly. They bring the client back to the body. They do not force clarity or push for emotional reactions. They allow space for whatever arises.

Spiritual trauma is a unique and often overlooked layer. Many people have been harmed in spiritual spaces through dogma, abuse of power, false prophecy, or manipulation. They may approach mediums with both hope and fear. They want to believe, but they also carry wounds.

A trauma-informed medium acknowledges this possibility. They do not demand trust. They earn it through integrity. They allow space for scepticism. They honour the client's right to question, to disagree, to hold doubt. They understand that spiritual healing must be grounded in emotional safety. Without that safety, even true messages can feel violating.

Mediums also carry their own trauma. This cannot be ignored. The unhealed wounds of the medium can bleed into the reading. They may overidentify with the client. They may project. They may seek validation through the reading. A trauma-informed medium does their own work. They are not perfect, but they are aware. They seek therapy, supervision, or mentorship. They reflect. They know their triggers. They do not use the reading to meet their own unmet needs. They take responsibility for their energy.

Trauma-informed mediumship is also about cultural humility. Trauma is shaped by race, gender, sexuality, class, and identity. The medium must be aware of their own position and privilege. They must listen to the lived experiences of others. They must be willing to unlearn. To recognize that what is true for them may not be true for the client. They must avoid universalizing spiritual truths.

A trauma-informed medium does not assume. They ask. They adapt. They honour the wisdom that each client brings.

The aftermath of a reading is also part of trauma-informed care. For some, a message may bring temporary relief followed by a deep emotional release. The medium does not vanish after the reading. They offer aftercare suggestions.

They may recommend journaling, rest, grounding practices, or professional support. They remind the client that it is okay to feel shaken. That healing is not always neat. They follow up if appropriate. They leave the door open for integration.

Being trauma-informed does not mean being afraid to speak truth. It means speaking truth with compassion. It means recognizing that the goal is not just to deliver a message but to support healing. Sometimes, the most healing act is not the message itself but the way it is held. The presence of the medium. Their willingness to sit in silence. To offer a tissue. To breathe together. To witness the tears without rushing to fix them.

This approach does not dilute mediumship. It deepens it. It roots it in humanity. It reminds us that spirit does not exist in a vacuum. It flows through human beings. Through pain and joy and complexity.

A trauma-informed medium does not see the client as a case. They see them as a soul in motion. A person navigating a difficult world. A sacred being worthy of tenderness.

Mediumship is a powerful tool. But like any tool, it can cause harm if misused. Trauma-informed practice is the ethical compass. It is the heart behind the skill. It is the soul of the work. It ensures that the messages given do not just land but heal. That the space created does not just impress but transform. That the medium does not just speak—but listens. Holds. Remembers what it means to be human.

And when this is done well, when the client leaves not only with a message but with a sense of being truly seen, truly held, something shifts. Not just in them, but in the world. The ripple begins. The healing expands and the medium, in their quiet, humble presence, becomes a sanctuary.

Reflection Questions: Trauma-Informed Mediumship – Holding Space for the Wounded Soul

1. Do I recognise when a message may be touching a traumatic memory, even if it arrives gently through spirit?

2. How do I hold emotional space for a sitter without trying to fix, rescue, or offer false comfort?

3. Am I aware of my own trauma triggers, and how they might subtly affect the way I deliver or interpret spirit messages?

4. What tools or practices help me regulate my nervous system before, during, and after emotionally intense sessions?

5. Can I sense when a sitter is overwhelmed and do I know how to pause, ground, or redirect when necessary?

6. Have I created a safe energetic container where the sitter feels respected, seen, and never judged?

7. How do I ensure that the words I speak from spirit are rooted in compassion, timing, and emotional intelligence?

8. Do I know the difference between emotional vulnerability and re-traumatisation and how do I honour that in my work?

9. What training, education, or self-study have I done to support trauma-informed awareness in my mediumship practice?

10. Have I ever witnessed spirit bring through a painful truth, and how did I choose to handle that ethically and responsibly?

11. When someone becomes emotional during a reading, do I become reactive, avoidant, or present and supportive?

12. What boundaries do I have in place to protect both the sitter and myself during high-emotion or trauma-laden sessions?

13. How do I decompress or cleanse after holding space for someone else's grief, pain, or unresolved trauma?

14. What language do I use that may unintentionally trigger someone and how can I refine my communication with sensitivity?

15. Do I truly believe that healing can begin through witnessing and how does that change how I show up in silence?

16. In what ways can I honour the trauma story without becoming entangled in it or letting it overshadow the soul message?

17. What is my relationship with silence, tears, or dissociation in a reading and how do I respond with gentleness and grounding?

18. Do I know when to suggest therapeutic support outside of mediumship and how do I do so with respect?

19. How has my own healing journey informed the way I hold space for others in pain?

20. If I were the wounded soul sitting across from me, what would I need most from the medium, not just the message, but the energy?

40. The Ongoing Path – Mediumship as a Lifelong Integration

Mediumship is not something you learn once and master forever. It is not a certificate you hang on your wall or a skill you perfect like playing an instrument. It is a living, breathing, evolving relationship with the unseen world. It is not just a practice. It is a way of being. It asks not only for your attention but your transformation. It challenges your beliefs, humbles your ego, opens your heart, and brings you face to face with death, grief, wonder, and truth.

There is no final destination in mediumship. There is only deepening. There is only becoming and this becoming lasts an entire lifetime, in this one and the next.

To integrate mediumship into your life is to walk the world with two hearts, one grounded in the human and the other attuned to the spirit. It means learning to live with sensitivity, with awareness, and with devotion. It means understanding that your journey as a medium is not separate from your journey as a person.

Your wounds, your healing, your growth, and your choices all shape the vessel through which the messages pass. The clearer and more whole you become as a person, the more truthful and compassionate you become as a medium. The path of mediumship does not pull you away from your humanity. It brings you more fully into it.

Lifelong integration requires ongoing reflection. The medium who believes they have nothing left to learn becomes stagnant. Every reading teaches something. Every silence reveals something.

Every connection with spirit has the power to shift your perspective. A true medium remains a student. Not because they are unskilled, but because they are wise enough to know that the universe cannot be mastered. It can only be listened to. Surrendered to. Walked with. The deeper the medium goes, the more they realize that the real mastery is in presence, not performance.

The integration of mediumship into daily life asks for rhythm. It is not sustainable to be open all the time.

A medium must learn to open and close. To enter and exit. To rest and to channel. There must be times for spirit and times for silence. Times for service and times for solitude.

The body and nervous system cannot handle constant spiritual exposure. Integration means creating rituals and practices that help you return to yourself after each reading. It means grounding, cleansing, eating, moving, connecting with nature. These are not luxuries. They are necessities. They allow the medium to remain strong, balanced, and able to show up with full presence.

Boundaries are a part of this lifelong integration. As the medium grows, their energetic sensitivity deepens. They may pick up on the emotions of others, feel overwhelmed in crowds, or struggle with fatigue. This is not a weakness. It is a call to deeper care. Boundaries are not walls. They are sacred agreements. They protect the gift.

They honour the vessel. A medium who integrates their gift learns when to say no, when to rest, when to listen, and when to walk away. They do not chase validation. They trust the rhythm of the work.

Integration also means weaving mediumship into identity in a way that feels whole. In the beginning, the gift may feel like something separate; a secret, a surprise, a skill that only comes out in sessions. Over time, it becomes a part of the self. It is not something you do. It is part of who you are. You begin to walk with a deeper knowing. You listen differently. You speak with more care. You live with more reverence. The veil between this world and the next becomes thinner, not only in your practice but in your presence.

There is also an emotional integration that occurs over time.

Mediums are often exposed to deep pain. Grieving parents. Lost children. Sudden deaths. Stories of trauma, regret, and longing. To hold space for this kind of emotion requires strength, but also softness.

A medium must learn to feel without becoming overwhelmed. They must learn to witness without taking on. This is a skill that deepens with practice. It is part of the lifelong path. The heart must remain open, but not porous. The soul must remain soft but not broken. The more the medium integrates their emotional body, the more resilient and grounded they become.

Integration includes continuing education. The spiritual world is vast. No one path holds all the answers. A medium who commits to lifelong growth will study psychology, culture, history, religion, healing, trauma, grief, energy work, and more. Not to become everything, but to deepen understanding. To meet clients with greater empathy. To recognize the many forms that spirit and healing can take. This kind of learning is not linear. It is spiral. Each new layer brings the medium deeper into wisdom, humility, and connection.

There will be seasons on the path. Times of great connection and times of silence. Times of certainty and times of doubt. Times when the medium feels like a clear channel, and times when they question everything. This is natural. The path of mediumship is not smooth. It is not predictable.

Every season has value. The winter teaches rest. The spring brings renewal. The summer brings full expression. The autumn teaches letting go. The integrated medium trusts the seasons. They do not panic when spirit goes quiet. They do not cling when spirit is loud. They ride the rhythm. They listen.

Over time, the medium becomes less concerned with proving and more devoted to serving. In the early stages, it is common to want to be right, to be accurate, to impress. As the medium integrates, those desires soften. The focus shifts from self to soul.

From ego to essence. The medium becomes a quiet force. A gentle presence. They do not need recognition. They need alignment. Their compass becomes internal.

Their worth is not tied to the number of clients, followers, or testimonials. It is tied to how they show up. With truth. With care. With love.

There is also a spiritual deepening that comes with integration. The medium's relationship with the unseen becomes more intimate. Not louder, but more nuanced. They begin to recognize different frequencies. They form deeper relationships with guides. They understand the symbolic language of the soul. They may receive messages not just for others, but for humanity. They may find themselves channelling, creating, writing, dreaming. The work expands. Not in volume, but in depth.

The medium becomes not just a reader, but a mystic. A healer. A messenger. A witness to something far greater.

The integrated medium also learns to live. To be here, fully, in the human world. To love. To play. To rest. To create. To grieve. To build a life that holds the sacred and the ordinary together. Mediumship is not about escaping this world. It is about living in it with deeper awareness. The spirit world does not ask us to transcend. It asks us to embody. To bring heaven to earth through how we live, love, and serve.

Over a lifetime, mediumship becomes less about messages and more about presence. People are drawn not only to the gift, but to the energy of the medium. The peace they carry. The wisdom they embody. The way they hold space. This is not performance. It is integration. It is the result of years of walking the path. Of doing the work. Of listening. Of healing. Of showing up again and again, even when it is hard.

There may be moments of great transformation. Illness. Loss. Awakening. These events shift the path. They bring new layers. The medium who is integrated does not resist. They surrender. They allow the work to evolve. They trust that the soul knows the way. They trust that the gift will grow as they do. They are not afraid of change. They are not afraid of stillness. They know that spirit moves in mysterious ways.

The lifelong path of mediumship is not always easy. It requires courage. Honesty. Vulnerability. But it is also rich with beauty. With wonder. With moments of connection that remind us why we chose this work. A mother hearing from her child. A father finally forgiving himself. A young woman remembering who she is. These moments are not small. They are sacred. They change lives.

And the medium, standing quietly in the middle, becomes a bridge between worlds.

To walk this path with integrity is to accept that it will challenge you. It will ask for your truth. It will strip away what is false. It will call you into deeper love, deeper service, deeper listening. And if you say yes, not just once, but again and again, you will find that mediumship becomes more than a practice. It becomes a way of being. A way of loving. A way of living.

You are not just a vessel. You are a soul. You are a witness to mystery. A keeper of sacred stories. A bridge between past and future, human and spirit, grief and healing.

Your work matters. Your presence matters. And your path, though often unseen, leaves a trail of light behind you.

This is the lifelong path of mediumship. Not always easy. But always sacred.

And the journey continues.

The Ongoing Path – Mediumship as a Lifelong Integration

50 Personal Reflection Questions for the Reader's Journey Forward

1. Who was I when I first opened this book and who am I now?

2. What beliefs about mediumship have shifted within me throughout this journey?

3. What parts of my story have been waiting to be witnessed, honoured, and reclaimed?

4. What old wounds still shape the way I show up as a spiritual being and a medium?

5. Where have I been silencing myself, and why?

6. Which chapter felt the most confronting for me, and what did it awaken?

7. Which chapter felt like coming home, and why?

8. What spiritual experiences from my past do I now understand in a new way?

9. What fears have I begun to release around being seen, heard, or fully present in my gift?

10. What does it mean to me now to be a *real* medium?

11. What aspects of my mediumship feel most natural, and which feel learned or performative?

12. How have my relationships with spirit changed as I've read and reflected?

13. What has this journey taught me about my inner child and their spiritual awareness?

14. In what ways has my body been calling out for healing, and have I started listening?

15. What does safety in spiritual practice truly feel like to me?

16. How do I now understand the relationship between trauma and spiritual sensitivity?

17. What parts of me have I judged, avoided, or bypassed in my mediumship practice?

18. What new practices or boundaries do I feel called to implement going forward?

19. What do I know now about the soul's role in grief, healing, and spirit communication?

20. When have I mistaken ego for intuition, and how can I recognise the difference more clearly now?

21. What does humility look like in my spiritual work?

22. What does energetic responsibility truly mean to me?

23. In what ways am I being invited to show up more courageously in service?

24. What ancestral echoes still live in me, and which ones am I ready to heal?

25. What sacred truth has been trying to rise from within me this entire time?

26. What spiritual archetype am I currently living, and what archetype am I evolving into?

27. Where am I still hiding?

28. Where am I finally ready to be seen?

29. What grief have I not yet fully allowed myself to feel, and why?

30. What would it look like to fully trust the silence from spirit as part of the process?

31. Where does shame still influence my voice, my energy, or my visibility as a medium?

32. What unique medicine do I bring to the world through my soul and my gift?

33. What does it mean for me to honour my boundaries as sacred, not selfish?

34. How does my body communicate with me during readings, and how do I honour its wisdom?

35. What spiritual rituals ground and restore me, and do I practice them regularly?

36. How does love, not fear, want to move through my work?

37. How do I repair and restore when I have made mistakes in spiritual service?

38. What would it mean to forgive myself for what I did not know then?

39. Who am I becoming, not just as a medium, but as a human?

40. What does legacy mean to me in the context of my mediumship?

41. If I died tomorrow, would I feel complete with the way I have honoured this gift?

42. What am I most proud of within myself after reading this book?

43. What is spirit still whispering to me that I have not yet acted on?

44. What commitment do I want to make to myself and my path today?

45. Where does my soul still long to go and what part of me holds the key?

46. What does an integrated, heart-centred mediumship practice look like for me now?

47. What am I afraid will happen if I fully live in my truth?

48. What would I lose, and what would I gain, if I trusted this path completely?

49. What do I want to leave behind here, and what do I want to carry forward?

50. If this book becomes the beginning of my next spiritual chapter, what do I name it?

DEAR SOUL TRAVELLER

Thank you for walking this journey with me. Thank you for opening not only this book, but your heart, your mind, your memories, and your spirit. It has been an honour to sit beside you across these pages, to share what I know, what I have lived, and what I have been shown through the grace of spirit and the wisdom of experience.

This book is not just mine. It belongs to every medium who has ever sat in the quiet and doubted their gift. To every soul who has wondered why their sensitivity feels like both a burden and a blessing. To every person who has questioned, wrestled, cried, loved, and chosen to keep going. It belongs to those who have served others from the edge of their own healing, who have felt the presence of spirit even when they could not explain it, and who have chosen to walk this path not for validation, but because they could not ignore the call.

You are not alone. I see you.

Mediumship is not a straight line. It is a spiral. A lifelong return to self. Some days it will flow like light through water. Other days it will go quiet. Some days you will feel the presence so clearly it takes your breath away. Other days, you will feel like you are grasping for echoes. Please do not mistake the silence for absence. Spirit is still there. Your gift is still alive, and you are still on the path.

If there is one thing I want to leave you with, it is this: your humanity is not a hindrance to your mediumship. It is the foundation of it. You do not need to leave your pain at the door to serve spirit. You do not need to be perfect. You only need to be present. Open. Honest. Willing. When you show up in truth, spirit does too. Every single time.

As you close this book, I invite you to take a breath. A deep one. And remember that this is not an ending. It is just the beginning, or perhaps a continuation of something ancient within you; something that has been waiting for this exact moment. You are here for a reason and you are reading these words for a reason. There is still so much ahead of you that spirit longs to show you, heal in you, and co-create with you.

Wherever you go from here, take this knowing with you: You are a vessel of light. A messenger of memory. A soul who dares to feel, to serve, to hold. That is rare. That is sacred and that is more than enough.

Being authentic IN your mediumship means being yourself truthfully without question.

With gratitude from the deepest part of my being, Thank you for letting me walk this part of your mediumship journey with you.

With love and deepest reverence,
Cameron Bayliss
6th Dimensional Medium